William Hamilton, S. S. Nelles

Chapters in Logic

Containing Sir William Hamilton's Lectures on Modified Logic and Selections from

the Port Royal Logic

William Hamilton, S. S. Nelles

Chapters in Logic
Containing Sir William Hamilton's Lectures on Modified Logic and Selections from the Port Royal Logic

ISBN/EAN: 9783337075194

Printed in Europe, USA, Canada, Australia, Japan

Cover: Foto ©Thomas Meinert / pixelio.de

More available books at **www.hansebooks.com**

CHAPTERS IN LOGIC;

CONTAINING

SIR WILLIAM HAMILTON'S LECTURES ON MODIFIED LOGIC,

AND SELECTIONS FROM

THE PORT ROYAL LOGIC.

WITH PREFACE
BY THE
REV. S. S. NELLES, D.D.,
Professor of Logic in Victoria College.

TORONTO:
THE WESLEYAN METHODIST BOOK-ROOM,
83, KING STREET EAST.

1870.

PREFACE.

THIS little volume is a reprint of Sir WILLIAM HAMILTON'S *Lectures on Modified Logic,* and of the most valuable portions of the famous *Port Royal Logic,* translated by T. S. BAYNES. The design of the publication is to provide, in cheap and convenient form, a Manual or Text-Book, on what Hamilton calls "Modified or Concrete Logic," but what others have variously designated as Applied or Practical Logic.

Whatever may be thought of the propriety of including this department of study within the science of Logic, there can be no doubt of its very great importance, and just as little doubt of its having been sadly neglected. Those who have not mastered the elements of formal or technical Logic, as well as those who have, may derive immense advantage from a careful perusal of these pages.

The merits of Sir William Hamilton are so well known, that it is perhaps unnecessary here to say anything in commendation of that part of the volume which was written by him. It may, however, be well to mention, that his *Lectures on Modified Logic* are here given in full, without alteration either of the arrangement or the text. From the nature of their topics, they form a distinct discussion in themselves, and suffer nothing in being separated from the other lectures in which the eminent author has so ably treated of the formal laws of thought.

The other work,—the *Port Royal Logic*,—is less generally known, but is regarded by high authorities as one of the very best of the many books extant on the science of Logic. "The treatise," says Mr. Baynes, "is characterised throughout by a vigor of thought, a vivacity of criticism, a freshness and variety of illustration, an honesty and love of truth, and withal a human sympathy, which rendered it a work not only of specific scientific value, but of general interest and instruction. Logic was thus redeemed from the contempt into which it had fallen, and placed on a level with the advancing philosophy of the time."

To this may be added the testimony of Baron de Gerando, as cited by Mr. Baynes. Speaking of the parts which especially merit praise, he says,—" Above all, that beautiful Dissertation on the Origin of Prejudices, and their influence on the vices of reasoning in civil life. This Dissertation, indeed, constitutes, of itself, an entirely new Logic —one almost sufficient, and far more important than all the apparatus of the peripatetic Logic; and it must be recorded to the praise of the Port Royal writers that this is a part of their work which is peculiarly their own."

Dugald Stewart, also, in his *Dissertation on the Progress of Philosophy*, speaks of the *Port Royal Logic* as "a treatise of which it is hardly possible to estimate the merits too highly." And again :—" No publication certainly, prior to *Locke's Essay*, can be named, containing so much good sense and so little nonsense on the science of Logic; and very few have *since* appeared on the same subject which can be justly preferred to it in point of practical utility. If the author had lived in the present age, or had been less fettered by a prudent regard to existing prejudices, the technical part would probably have been reduced within a still narrower compass; but even there he has contrived to substitute, for the puerile and contemptible examples of common logicians, several interesting illustrations from the physical discoveries of his immediate predecessors; and has indulged himself in some short excursions, which excite a lively regret that he has not more frequently and freely given scope to his original reflections. Among these excursions, the most valuable, in my opinion, is *the Twentieth Chapter of the Third Part*, which deserves the attention of every logical student, as an important and instructive supplement to the enumeration of sophisms given by Aristotle."

The Editor of this compilation has confined his selections from the *Port Royal Logic* to this "twentieth chapter," which is given entire (with the exception of a few lines), and to those portions of the Preliminary Discourse which are of general application. These selections make a suitable introduction to the Lectures of Hamilton on *Modified Logic*, and the two together furnish about the best instruction that can be had on this important branch of the science of Logic.

We live in times remarkable for the awakening and emancipation of thought. This is matter of rejoicing; but freedom of thought brings 'esponding dangers and responsibilities, and we cannot do too much to aid the inquiring multitudes in the proper use of that right of private judgment of which we are so justly proud. Works like the one here presented may serve to show that all intellectual activity has its laws, the violation of which brings invariable and heavy penalties; may teach us to beware of the immoralities of the intellect; may put those who are trying to think, in the way of thinking soundly, by furnishing them with the best rules and cautions known to the world's great thinkers; and may help us forward to that "good time coming," when in moral, political, and religious affairs, men shall proceed with something like the steadiness, precision, and certainty, which have already begun to mark the pursuit of mathematical and physical science.

VICTORIA COLLEGE,
March 31*st*, 1870.

THE PORT-ROYAL LOGIC

CHAPTER I.

PRELIMINARY—IN WHICH THE DESIGN OF THIS NEW LOGIC IS SET FORTH.

THERE is nothing more desirable than good sense, and accuracy of thought, in discriminating between truth and falsehood. All other qualities of mind are of limited use; but exactness of judgment is of general utility in every part, and in all the employments of life. It is not alone in the sciences that it is difficult to distinguish truth from error, but also in the greater part of those subjects which men discuss in their every-day affairs. There are, in relation to almost everything, different routes—the one true, the other false—and it is reason which must choose between them. Those who choose well, are they who have minds well-regulated; those who choose ill, are those who have minds ill-regulated: and this is the first and most important difference which we find between the qualities of men's minds.

Thus the main object of our attention should be, to form our judgment, and render it as exact as possible; and to this end, the greater part of our study ought to tend. We employ reason as an instrument for acquiring the sciences; whereas, on the contrary, we ought to avail ourselves of the sciences as an instrument for perfecting our reason—justness of mind being infinitely more important than all the speculative knowledges which we can obtain, by means of sciences the most solid and well-established. This ought to lead wise men to engage in these only so far as they may contribute to that end, and to make them the exercise only, and not the occupation, of their mental powers.

If we have not this end in view, the study of the speculative science—such as geometry, astronomy, and physics—will be little else than a vain amusement, and scarcely better than the ignorance of these things, which has at least this advantage—that it is less laborious, and affords no room for that empty vanity which is often found connected with these barren and unprofitable knowledges. These sciences not only have nooks and hidden places of very little use; they are even totally useless, considered in themselves, and for themselves alone. Men are not born to employ their time in measuring lines, in examining the relations of angles, and considering the different movements of matter; their minds are too great, their life too short, their time too precious, to be engrossed with such petty objects: but they ought to be just, equitable, prudent, in all their converse, in all their actions, and in all the business they transact; and to these things they ought specially to discipline and train themselves. This care and study are so very neccessary, that it is strange that this exactness of judgment should be so rare a quality. We find, on every side, ill-regulated minds which have scarcely any discernment of the truth; men who receive all things with a wrong bias; who allow themselves to be carried away by the slightest appearances; who are always in excess and extremes; who have no bond to hold them firm to the truths which they know, since they are attached to them rather by chance than by any clear insight; or who, on the other hand, entrench themselves in their opinions with such obstinacy, that they will not listen to anything that may undeceive them; who determine rashly about that of which they are ignorant, which they do not understand, and which, perhaps, no one ever can understand; who make no difference between one speech and another, or judge of the truth of things by the tone of voice alone,—he who speaks fluently and impressively being in the right, he who has some difficulty in explaining himself, or displays some warmth, in the wrong: they know nothing beyond this.

Hence it is, that there are no absurdities too groundless to find supporters. Whoever determines to deceive the world, may be sure of finding people who are willing enough to be deceived; and the most absurd follies always find minds to which they are adapted. After seeing what a number are infatuated with the follies of judicial astrology, and that even grave persons treat this subject seriously, we need not be surprised at anything more. There is a constellation in the heavens which it has pleased certain persons to call the Balance, and which is as much like a balance as a windmill. The Balance is the symbol of justice; those, therefore, that are born under that constellation, will be just and equitable. There are three other signs in the zodiac, which are called, one the Ram, another the Bull, another the Goat, and which might as well have been called the Elephant, the Crocodile, and the Rhinoceros. The Ram, the Bull, and the Goat, are ruminant animals; those, therefore, who take medicines when the moon is under these constellations, are in danger of vomiting them again. Such extravagant reasonings as these have found persons to propagate them, and others who allow themselves to be persuaded by them.

This inaccuracy of thought is the cause, not only of the errors we meet with in the sciences, but also the majority of the offences which are committed in civil life,—of unjust quarrels, unfounded lawsuits, rash counsel, and ill-arranged undertakings. There are few of these which have not their origin in some error, and in some fault of judgment, so that there is no defect which it more concerns us to correct. But this correction is as difficult of accomplishment as it is desirable, since it depends very much on the measure of intelligence with which we are endowed. Common-sense is not so common a quality as we imagine. There are a multitude of minds heavy and dull, which we cannot reform by giving them the understanding of the truth, but only by restricting them to those things which are suited to them, by withholding them from judging about those things which they are not capable of knowing. It is true, nevertheless, that a great part of the false judgment of men does not spring from this principle, but is caused solely by precipitancy of mind and want of attention, which lead us to judge rashly about that which we know only obscurely and confusedly. The little love men have for truth leads them to take no pains, for the most part, in distinguishing what is true from what is false. They allow all sorts of reasonings and maxims to enter their minds; they like better to suppose things true, than to examine them; if they do not comprehend them, they are willing to believe that others understand them well: and thus they fill the memory with a mass of things false, obscure, and unintelligible, and then reason on these principles, scarcely considering at all either what they speak or what they think. Vanity and presumption contribute still more to this effect. We think it a disgrace to doubt, and to be ignorant; and we prefer rather to speak and determine at random, than to confess that we are not sufficiently informed on the subject to give an opinion. We are all of us full of ignorance and errors; and yet it is the most difficult thing in the world to obtain from the lips of man this confession, so just, and so suited to his natural state,—I am in error, and I know nothing about the matter.

We find others, on the contrary, who, having light enough to know that there are a number of things obscure and uncertain, and wishing, from another kind of vanity, to show that they are not led away by the popular credulity, take a pride in maintaining that there is nothing certain. They thus free themselves from the labour of examination, and on this evil principle they bring into doubt the most firmly established truths, and even religion itself. This is the source of Pyrrhonism [or Scepticism], another extravagance of the human mind which, though apparently opposed to the rashness of those who believe and decide everything, springs nevertheless from the same source, which is, want of attention. For as the one will not give themselves the trouble of discerning errors, the others will not look upon truth with that care which is necessary to perceive its evidence. The faintest glimmer suffices to persuade the one of things very false, and to make the other doubt of things the most certain; and in both cases it is the same want of application which produces effects so different.

True reason places all things in the rank which belongs to them; it questions those which are doubtful, rejects those which are false, and acknowledges, in good faith, those which are evident, without being embarrassed by the vain reasons of the Pyrrhonists, which never could, even in the minds of those who proposed them, destroy the reasonable assurance we have of many things. None ever seriously doubted the existence of the sun, the earth, the moon, or that the whole was greater than its parts. We may indeed easily say outwardly with the lips that we doubt of all these things, because it is possible for us to lie; but we cannot say this in our hearts. Thus Pyrrhonism is not a sect composed of men who are persuaded of what they say, but a sect of liars. Hence they often contradict themselves in uttering their opinion, since it is impossible for their hearts to agree with their language. We see this in Montaigne, who attempted to revive this sect in the last century; for, after having said that the Academics were different from the Pyrrhonists, inasmuch as the Academics maintained that some things were more probable than others, which the Pyrrhonists would not allow, he declares himself on the side of the Pyrrhonists in the following terms: "The opinion," says he, "of the Pyrrhonists is bolder, and much more probable." There are, therefore, some things which are more probable than others. Nor was it for the sake of effect that he spoke thus: these are words which escaped him without thinking of them, springing from the depths of nature which no illusion of opinions can destroy. But the evil is, that in relation to those things which are more removed from sense, these persons, who take a pleasure in doubting everything, withhold their mind from any application, or apply it only imperfectly to that which might persuade them, and thus fall into a voluntary uncertainty in relation to the affairs of religion; for the state of darkness into which they have brought themselves is agreeable to them, and very favourable for allaying the remorse of their conscience, and for the unrestrained indulgence of their passions. Thus, these disorders of the mind, though apparently opposed (the one leading to the inconsiderate belief of what is obscure and uncertain, the other to the doubting of what is clear and certain), have nevertheless a common origin, which is, the neglect of that attention which is necessary in order to discover the truth. It is clear, therefore, that they must also have a common remedy, and that the only way in which we can preserve ourselves from them is by fixing minute attention on our judgments and thoughts. This is the only thing that is absolutely necessary to preserve us from deceptions. For that which the Academics were wont to say,—that it was impossible to discover the truth unless we had its characters, as it would be impossible to identify a runaway slave we might be in search of, unless we had some signs by which, supposing we were to meet him, we could distinguish him from others,—is only a vain subtlety. As no marks are necessary in order to distinguish light from darkness but the light which reveals itself, so nothing else is necessary in order to recognize the truth but the very brightness which environs it, and which subdues and persuades the mind, notwithstanding all that may be said against it; so that all the reasonings of these philosophers are no more able to withhold the mind from yielding to the truth, when it is strongly imbued with it, than they are capable of preventing the eyes from seeing, when, being open, they are assailed by the light of the sun.

But since the mind often allows itself to be deceived by false appearances in consequence of not giving due attention to them, and since there are many things which cannot be known, save by long and difficult examination, it would certainly be useful to have some rules for its guidance, so that the search after truth might be more easy and certain. Nor is it impossible to secure such rules: for since men are sometimes deceived in their judgments, and at other times are not deceived, as they reason sometimes well and sometimes ill, and as, after they have reasoned ill, they are able to perceive their error, they may thus notice, by reflecting on their thoughts, what method they have followed when they have reasoned well, and what was the cause of their error when they were deceived; and thus on these reflections form rules by which they may avoid being deceived for the future.

This is what philosophers have specially undertaken to accomplish, and in relation to which they make such magnificent promises. If we may believe them, they will furnish us, in that part which is devoted to that purpose, and which they call *logic*, with a light capable of dispelling all the darkness of the mind; they correct all the errors of our thoughts; and they give us rules so sure that they conduct us infallibly to the truth,—so necessary, that without them it is impossible to know anything with complete certainty. These are the praises which they have themselves bestowed on their precepts. But if we consider what experience shows us of the use which these philosophers make of them, both in logic and in other parts of philosophy, we shall have good grounds to suspect the truth of their promises.

Since it is not, however, just to reject absolutely the good there is in logic because of the abuse which has been made of it, and as it is not possible that all the great minds which have applied themselves with so much care to the rules of reasoning, have discovered nothing at all solid; and finally, since custom has rendered it necessary to know (at least generally) what logic is, we believed that it would contribute something to public utility to select from the common logics whatever might best help towards forming the judgment. This is the end we specially propose to ourselves in this work ; with the view of accomplishing which, we have inserted many new reflections which have suggested themselves to our mind while writing it, and which form the greatest and perhaps the most important part of it, for it appears the common philosophers have attempted to do little more than to give the rules of good and bad reasoning. Now, although we cannot say these rules are useless, since they often help to discover the vice of certain intricate arguments, and to arrange our thoughts in a more convincing manner, still this utility must not be supposed to extend very far. The greater part of the errors of men arise, not from their allowing themselves to be deceived by wrong conclusions, but in their proceeding from false judgments, whence wrong conclusions are deduced. Those who have previously written on logic have little sought to rectify this, which is the main design of the new reflections which are to be found scattered through this book.

These, in brief, are the views we have had in writing this Logic. Perhaps, after all there are few persons who will profit by it, or be conscious of the good they have obtained, because but little attention is commonly given to putting precepts in practice by express reflections on them. But we hope, nevertheless, that those who have read it with some care may receive an impression which will render them more exact and solid in their judgments, even without their being conscious of the good, as there are some remedies

2*

which cure diseases by increasing the vigour and fortifying the parts. Be this as it may, it cannot trouble any one long,—since those who are a little advanced may read and understand it in seven or eight days ; and it will be strange if, containing so great a diversity of things, each does not find something to repay him for the trouble of a perusal.

CHAPTER II.

OF THE BAD REASONINGS WHICH ARE COMMON IN CIVIL LIFE AND IN ORDINARY DISCOURSE.

WE have seen some examples of the faults which are most common in reasoning on scientific subjects; but since the principal use of reason is not in relation to those kinds of subjects which enter but little into the conduct of life, and in which there is much less danger of being deceived, it would, without doubt, be much more useful to consider generally what betrays men into the false judgments which they make on every kind of subject,—especially on that of morals, and of other things which are important in civil life, and which constitute the ordinary subject of their conversation. But, inasmuch as this design would require a separate work, which would comprehend almost all the whole of morals, we shall content ourselves with indicating here, in general, some of the causes of those false judgments which are so common amongst men.

We do not stay to distinguish false judgments from bad reasonings, and shall inquire indifferently into the causes of each,—both because false judgments are the sources of bad reasonings, and produce them as a necessary consequence, and because in reality there is almost always a concealed and enveloped reasoning in what appears to be a simple judgment, there being always something which operates on the motive and principle of that judgment. For example, when we judge that a stick which appears bent in the water is really so, this judgment is founded on that general and false proposition, that what appears bent to our senses is so really, and thus contains an undeveloped reasoning.

In considering them generally, the causes of our errors appear to be reducible to two principles: the one internal —the *irregularity of the will,* which *troubles and disorders the judgment;* the other external, which lies in the *objects of which we judge,* and which deceive our minds by *false appearances.* Now although these causes almost always appear united together, there are nevertheless certain errors, in which one prevails more than the other; and hence we shall treat of them separately.

OF THE SOPHISMS OF SELF-LOVE, OF INTEREST, AND OF PASSION.

I.

If we examine with care what commonly attaches men rather to one opinion than to another, we shall find that it is not a conviction of the truth, and the force of the reasons, but some bond of self-love, of interest, or of passion. This is the weight which bears down the scale, and which decides us in the greater part of our doubts. It is this which gives the greatest impetus to our judgments, and which holds us to them most forcibly. We judge of things, not by what they are in themselves, but by what they are in relation to us, and truth and utility are to us but one and the same thing.

No other proofs are needed than those which we see every day, to show that the things which are held everywhere else as doubtful, or even as false, are considered most certain by all of some one nation, or profession, or institution. For, since it cannot be that what is true in Spain should be false in France, nor that the minds of all Spaniards are so differently constituted from those of Frenchmen, as that, judging by the same rules of reasoning, that which appears generally true to the one should appear generally false to the others, it is plain that this diversity of judgment can arise from no other cause except that the one choose to hold as true that which is to their advantage ; and that the others, having no interest at stake, judge of it in a different way.

Nevertheless, what can be more unreasonable than to take our interest as the motive for believing a thing ? All that it can do, at most, is to lead us to consider with more attention the reasons which may enable us to discover the truth of that which we wish to be true ; but it is only the truth which must be found in the thing itself, independently of our desires, which ought to convince us. I am of such a country ; therefore I must believe that such a saint preached the gospel there. I am of such an order ; therefore I must believe that such a privilege is right. These are no reasons. Of whatever order, and of whatever country you may be, you ought to believe only what is true ; and what you would have been disposed to believe, though you had been of another country, of another order, and of another profession.

II.

But this illusion is much more evident when any change takes place in the passions ; for, though all things remain in their place, it appears, nevertheless, to those who are moved by some new passion, that the change which has taken place in their own heart alone has changed all external things which have any relation to them. How often do we see persons who are able to recognize no good quality, either natural or acquired, in those against whom they have conceived an aversion, or who have been opposed in something to their feelings, desires, and interests! This is enough to render them at once, in their estimation, rash, proud, ignorant, without faith, without honour, and without conscience. Their affections and desires are not any more just or moderate than their hatred. If they love any one, he is free from every kind of defect. Everything which they desire is just and easy, everything which they do not desire is unjust and impossible, without their being able to assign any other reason for all these judgments than the passion itself which possesses them; so that, though they do not expressly realize to their mind this reasoning: I love him; therefore, he is the cleverest man in the world: I hate him; therefore, he is nobody;—they realize it to a great extent in their hearts; and therefore, we may call sophisms and delusions of the heart those kinds of errors which consist in transferring our passion to the objects of our passions, and in judging that they are what we will or desire that they should be; which is without doubt very unreasonable, since our desires can effect no change in the existence of that which is without us, and since it is God alone whose will is efficacious enough to render all things what he would have them to be.

III.

We may reduce to the same illusion of self-love that of those who decide everything by a very general and convenient principle, which is, that they are right, that they know the truth; from which it is not difficult to infer that those who are not of their opinion are deceived,—in fact, the conclusion is necessary.

The error of these persons springs solely from this, that the good opinion which they have of their own insight leads them to consider all their thoughts as so clear and evident, that they imagine the whole world must accept them as soon as they are known. Hence it is that they so rarely trouble themselves to furnish proofs,—they seldom listen to the opinions of others, they wish all to yield to their authority, since they never distinguish their authority from reason. They treat with contempt all those who are not of their opinion, without considering that if others are not of their opinion, so neither are they of the opinion of others, and that it is unjust to assume, without proof, that we are in the right when we attempt to convince others, who are not of our opinion, simply because they are persuaded that we are not in the right.

IV.

There are some, again, who have no other ground for rejecting certain opinions than this amusing reasoning :— If this were so, I should not be a clever man ; now, I am a clever man ; therefore, it is not so. This is the main reason which, for a long time, led to the rejection of some most useful remedies, and most certain discoveries ; for those who had not known them previously fancied that, by admitting them, they would have confessed themselves to have been hitherto deceived. "What," said they, "if the blood circulate; if the food is not carried to the liver by the mesaraic veins ; if the venous artery carry the blood to the heart; if the blood rise by the descending hollow vein ; if nature does not abhor a vacuum ; if the air be heavy and have a movement below,—I have been ignorant of many important things in anatomy and in physics.

these things, therefore, cannot be." But, to remedy this folly, it is only necessary to represent fully to such, that there is very little discredit in being mistaken, and that they may be accomplished in other things, though they be not in those which have been recently discovered.

V.

There is, again, nothing more common than to see people mutually casting on each other the same reproaches, and accusing one another—for example, of obstinacy, passion, and chicanery—when they are of different opinions. There are scarcely any advocates who do not accuse each other of delaying the process, and concealing the truth by artifices of speech; and thus those who are in the right, and those who are in the wrong, with almost the same language make the same complaints, and attribute to each other the same vices. This is one of the most injurious things possible in the life of men, for it throws truth and error, justice and injustice, into an obscurity so profound, that the world, in general, cannot distinguish between them; and hence it happens, that many attach themselves, by chance and without knowledge, to one of these parties, and that others condemn both as being equally wrong.

All this confusion springs, again, from the same malady which leads each one to take, as a principle, that he is in the right; for from this it is not difficult to infer, that all who oppose us are obstinate, since to be obstinate is not to submit to the right.

But still, although it be true that these reproaches of passion, of blindness, and of quibbling, which are very unjust on the part of those who are mistaken, are just and right on the part of those who are not so; nevertheless, since they assume that truth is on the side of him who makes them, wise and thoughtful persons, who treat of any contested matter, should avoid using them, before they have thoroughly established the truth and justice of the cause which they maintain. They will never then accuse their adversaries of obstinacy, of rashness, of wanting common sense, before they have clearly proved this. They will not say, before they have shown it, that they fall into intolerable absurdities and extravagances; for the others, on their side, will say the same of them, and thus accomplish nothing. And thus they will prefer rather to observe that most equitable rule of St. Augustine:—*Omittamus ista communia, quæ dici ex utraque parte possunt, licet vere dici ex utraque parte non possint.* They will thus be content to defend truth by the weapons which are her own, and which falsehood cannot borrow. These are clear and weighty reasons.

VI.

The mind of man is not only in love with itself, but it is also naturally jealous, envious of and ill-disposed towards others. It can scarcely bear that they should have any advantage, but desires it all for itself; and as it is an advantage to know the truth, and furnish men with new views, a secret desire arises to rob those who do this of the glory, which often leads men to combat, without reason, the opinions and inventions of others.

Thus, as self-love often leads us to make these ridiculous reasonings: It is an opinion which I discovered, it is that of my order, it is an opinion which is convenient; it is, therefore, true; natural ill-will leads us often to make these others, which are equally absurd: Some one else said such a thing; it is, therefore, false: I did not write that book; it is, therefore, a bad one.

This is the source of the spirit of contradiction so common amongst men, and which leads them, when they hear or read anything of another, to pay but little attention to the reasons which might have persuaded them, and to think only of those which they think may be offered against it; they are always on their guard against truth, and think only of the means by which it may be repressed and obscured—in which they are almost invariably successful, the fertility of the human mind in false reasons being inexhaustible.

When this vice is in excess, it constitutes one of the leading characteristics of the spirit of pedantry, which finds its greatest pleasure in quibbling with others on the pettiest things, and in contradicting everything with a pure malignity. But it is often more imperceptible and concealed; and we may say, indeed, that no one is altogether free from it, since it has its root in self-love, which always lives in men.

The knowledge of this malignant and envious disposition, which dwells deep in the heart of men, shows us that one of the most important rules which we can observe, in order to win those to whom we speak from error, and bring them over to the truth of which we would persuade them, is to excite their envy and jealousy as little as possible by speaking of ourselves, and the things which concern us.

For, since men love scarcely any but themselves, they cannot bear that another should intrude himself upon them, and thus throw into shade the main object of their regard. All that does not refer to themselves is odious and impertinent, and they commonly pass from the hatred of the man to the hatred of his opinions and reasons. Hence, wise persons avoid as much as possible revealing to others the advantages which they have; they avoid attracting attention to themselves in particular; and seek rather, by hiding themselves in the crowd, to escape observation, in order that the truth which they propose may be seen alone in their discourse.

The late M. Pascal, who knew as much of true rhetoric as any one ever did, carried this rule so far as to maintain that a well-bred man ought to avoid mentioning himself, and even to avoid using the words *I* and *me;* and he was accustomed to say, on this subject, that Christian piety annihilated the human *me*, and that human civility concealed and suppressed it. This rule, however, is not to be observed too rigidly, for there are many occasions on which it would uselessly embarrass us to avoid these words; but it is always good to keep it in view, in order to preserve us from the wretched custom of some individuals, who speak only of themselves, and who quote themselves continually, when their opinion is not asked for. This leads those who hear them to suspect that this constant recurrence to themselves arises only from a secret pleasure, which leads them continually to that object of their love, and thus excites in them, by a natural consequence, a secret aversion to these people, and towards all that they say. This shows us that one of the characteristics most unworthy of a sensible man is that which Montaigne has affected in entertaining his readers with all his humours, his inclinations, his fancies, his maladies, his virtues, and his vices, which could arise only from a weakness of judgment, as well as a violent love for himself. It is true that he attempted, as far as possible, to remove from himself the suspicion of a low and vulgar vanity, by speaking freely of his defects, as well as of his good qualities, which has something amiable in it, from the appearance of sincerity; but it is easy to see that all this is only a trick and artifice; which should only render it still more odious. He speaks of his vices in order that they may be known, not that they may be detested; he does not think for a moment that he ought to be held in less esteem; he regards them as things very indifferent, and rather as creditable than disgraceful; if he reveals them it gives him no concern, and he believes that he will not be, on that account, at all more vile or contemptible. But when he apprehends that anything will degrade him at all, he is as careful as any one to conceal it; hence, a celebrated author of the present day pleasantly remarks, that though he takes great pains, without any occassion, to inform us, in two places of his book, that he had a page, (an officer of very little use in the house of a gentleman of six thousand livres a-year) he has not taken the same pains to inform us that he had also a clerk, having been himself counsellor of the parliament of Bordeaux. This employment, though very honourable in itself, did not satisfy the vanity he had of appearing always with the air of a gentleman and of a cavalier, and as one unconnected with the brief and gown.

It is nevertheless probable, however, that he would not have concealed this circumstance of his life if he could have found some Marshal of France who had been counsellor of Bordeaux, as he has chosen to inform us that he had been mayor of that town, but only, after having informed us that he had succeeded Marshal De Biron in that office, and had been succeeded by Marshal De Matignon.

But the greatest vice of this author is not that of vanity, for he is filled with such a multitude of shameful scandals, and of epicurean and impious maxims, that it is wonderful that he has been endured so long by everybody, and that there are even men of mind who have not discovered the poison.

No other proofs are necessary, in order to judge of his libertinism, than that very manner even in which he speaks of his vices; for allowing, in many places, that he had been guilty of a great number of criminal excesses, he declares, nevertheless, that he did not repent of them at all, and that if he had to live over again he would live as he had done. "As for me," says he, "I cannot desire in general to be other than I am. I cannot condemn my universal form, though I may be displeased with it, and pray God for my entire reformation, and for the pardon of my natural weakness; but this I ought not to call repentance any more than the dissatisfaction I may feel at not being an angel, or Cato; my actions are regulated and conformed to my state and condition; I cannot be better, and repentance does not properly refer to things which are not in our power. I never expected incongruously to affix the tail of a philosopher to the head and body of an abandoned man, or that the meagre extremity of my life was to disavow and deny the most beautiful, complete, and largest portion of the whole. If I had to live over again I would live as I have done; I do not lament over the past; I do not fear for the future." Awful words, which denote the entire extinction of all religious feeling, but which are worthy of him who said also, in another place: "I plunge myself headlong blindly into death, as into a dark and silent abyss, full of a mighty sleep, full of unconsciousness and lethargy, which engulphs me at once, and overwhelms me in a moment." And in another place: "Death, which is only a quarter of an hour's passion, without consequence, and without injury, does not deserve any special precepts."

Although this digression appears widely removed from this subject, it belongs to it nevertheless, for this reason—that there is no book which more fosters that bad custom of speaking of one's self, being occupied with one's self, and wishing all others to be so too. This wonderfully corrupts reason, both in ourselves, through the vanity which always accompanies these discourses, and in others, by the contempt and aversion which they conceive for us. Those only may be allowed to speak of themselves who are men of eminent virtue, and who bear witness by what means they have become so, so that if they make known their good actions, it is only to excite others to praise God for these, or to instruct them; and if they publish their faults, it is only to humble themselves before men, and to deter them from committing these. But for ordinary persons it is a ridiculous vanity to wish to inform others of their petty advantages; and it is insufferable effrontery to reveal their excesses to the world without expressing their sorrow for them, since the last degree of abandonment in vice is, not to blush for it, and to have no concern or repentance on account of it, but to speak of it indifferently as of anything else; in which mainly lies the wit of Montaigne.

VII.

We may distinguish to some extent from malignant and envious contradiction another kind of disposition not so bad, but which produces the same faults of reasoning; this is the spirit of debate, which is, however, a vice very injurious to the mind.

It is not that discussions, generally, can be censured. We may say on the contrary that, provided they be rightly used, there is nothing which contributes more towards giving us different hints, both for finding the truth, and for recommending it to others. The movement of the mind, when it works alone in the examination of any subject, is commonly too cold and languid. It needs a certain warmth to inspire it, and awaken its ideas, and it is commonly through the varied opposition which we meet with that we discover wherein the obscurity and the difficulties of conviction consist, and are thus led to endeavor to overcome them.

It is true, however, that just in proportion as this exercise is useful when we employ it aright, and without any mixture of passion, so, in that proportion, is it dangerous when we abuse it, and pride ourselves on maintaining our opinion at whatever cost, and in contradicting that of others. Nothing can separate us more widely from the truth, and plunge us more readily into error, than this kind of disposition. We become accustomed, unconsciously, to find reasons for everything, and to place ourselves above reason by never yielding to it, which leads us by degrees to hold nothing as certain, and to confound truth with error, in regarding both as equally probable. This is why it is so rare a thing for a question to be determined by discussion; and why it scarcely ever happens that two philosophers agree. They always find replies and rejoinders, since their aim is to avoid not error but silence, and since they think it less disgraceful to remain always in error than to avow that they are mistaken.

Thus, unless at least we have been accustomed by long discipline to retain the perfect mastery over ourselves, it is very difficult not to lose sight of truth in debates, since there are scarcely any exercises which so much arouse our passions. What vices have they not excited, says a celebrated author [Montaigne], being almost always governed by anger! We pass first to a hatred of the reasons, and then of the persons. We learn to dispute only to contradict; and each contradicting and being contradicted, it comes to pass that the result of the debate is the annihilation of truth. One goes to the east and another to the west—one loses the principle in dispute, and another wanders amidst a crowd of details—and after an hour's storm, they know not what they were discussing. One is above, another below, and another at the side—one seizes on a word or similitude—another neither listens to, nor at all understands what his opponent says, and is so engaged with his own course that he only thinks of following himself, not you.

There are some, again, who, conscious of their weakness, fear everything, refuse everything, confuse the discussion at the onset, or in the midst of it, become obstinate, and are silent, affecting a proud contempt, or a stupid modesty of avoiding contention. One, provided only that he is striking, cares not how he exposes himself—another counts his words and weighs his reasons—a third relies on his voice and lungs alone. We see some who conclude against themselves, and others who weary and bewilder everyone with prefaces and useless digressions. Finally, there are some who arm themselves with abuse, and make a German quarrel in order to finish the dispute with one who has worsted them in argument. These are the common vices of our debates, which are ingeniously enough represented by this writer,* who, without ever having known the true grandeur of man, has sufficiently canvassed his defects.

---

* The greater part of this page is taken directly from Montaigne, *Essays* iii. 8. His sentiments are here referred to with approbation; and it would have been but fair, since when quoted for condemna-

We may hence judge how liable these kinds of conferences are to disorder the mind, at least unless we take great care not only not to fall ourselves first into these errors, but also not to follow those who do, and so to govern ourselves that we may see them wander without wandering ourselves, and without losing the end we ought to seek, which is the elucidation of the truth under discussion.

VIII.

We find some persons, again, principally amongst those who attend at court, who, knowing very well how inconvenient and disagreeable these controversial dispositions are, adopt an immediately opposite course, which is that of contradicting nothing, but of praising and approving everything indifferently. This is what is called complaisance, which is a disposition convenient enough indeed for our fortune, but very injurious to our judgment, for as the controversial hold as true the contrary of what is said to them, the complaisant appear to take as true everything which is said to them, and this habit corrupts, in the first place, their discourse, and then their minds.

Hence it is that praises are become so common, and are given so indifferently to everyone, that we know not what to conclude from them. There is not a single preacher in the "Gazette," who is not most eloquent, and who does not ravish his hearers by the profundity of his knowledge. Al who die are illustrious for piety; and the pettiest authors

---

tion he is always mentioned by name, that he should here also have been expressly referred to. The gay and easy scepticism of Montaigne, however, so offended the moral earnestness of the Port-Royal writers, that they can scarcely allow him any merit; and rarely, when referring to him, do him justice.

might make books of praises which they receive from their friends. So that, amidst this profusion of praises, which are made with such little discernment, it is matter of wonder that there are found some so eager for them, and who treasure them so carefully when given.

It is quite impossible that this confusion in the language should not produce some confusion in the mind, for those who adopt the habit of praising everything, become accustomed also to approve of everything. But though the falsehood were only in the words, and not in the mind, this would be sufficient to lead those who sincerely love the truth to avoid it. It is not necessary to reprove everything which may be bad, but it is necessary to praise only what is truly praiseworthy, otherwise we lead those whom we praise in this way into error. We help to deceive those who judge of their persons by these praises; and we commit a wrong against those who truly deserve praises, by giving them equally to those who do not deserve them. Finally, we destroy all the trustworthiness of language, and confuse all ideas and words, by causing them to be no longer signs of our judgments and thoughts, but simply an outward civility which we give to those whom we praise as we might do a bow, for this is all that we can infer from ordinary praises and compliments.

IX.

Amongst the various ways by which self-love plunges men into error, or rather strengthens them in it, and prevents their escape from it, we must not forget one which is without doubt among the principal and most common. This is the engaging to maintain any opinion, to which we may attach ourselves from other considerations than those of its truth. For this determination to defend our opinion leads us no longer to consider whether the reasons we employ are true or false, but whether they will avail to defend that which we maintain. We employ all sorts of reasons, good or bad, in order that there may be some to suit every one; and we sometimes proceed even to say things which we well know to be absolutely false, if they will contribute to the end which we seek. The following are some examples:—

An intelligent man would hardly ever suspect Montaigne of having believed all the dreams of judicial astrology. Nevertheless, when he needs them for the purpose of foolishly degrading mankind, he employs them as good reasons. "When we consider," says he, "the dominion and power which these bodies have, not only on our lives, and on the state of our fortune, but also on our inclinations, which are governed, driven, and disturbed, according to their influences, how can we deprive them of a soul, of life, and of discourse?"

Would he destroy the advantages which men have over beasts through the intercourse of speech, he relates to us absurd stories, whose extravagance no one knew better than himself, and derives from them these still more absurd conclusions:—"There have been," says he, "some who boasted that they understood the language of brutes, as Appollonious Thyaneous, Melampus, Tiresias, Thales, and others; and since what the cosmographers say is true, that there are some nations which receive a dog as their king, they must give a certain interpretation to his voice and movements." [Essays, ii. 12.]

We might conclude, for the same reason, that when Caligula made his horse consul, the orders which he gave in the discharge of that office must have been clearly understood. But we should do wrong in accusing Montaigne of this bad consequence; his design was not to speak reasonably, but to gather together a confused mass of everything which might be said against men, which is, however, a vice utterly opposed to the justness of mind and sincerity of a good man.

Who, again, would tolerate this other reasoning of the same author on the subject of the auguries which the pagans made from the flight of birds, and which the wisest amongst them derided? "Amongst all the predictions of time past," says he, "the most ancient, and the most certain, were those which were derived from the flight of birds. We have nothing of the like kind—nothing so admirable; that rule, that order of the moving of the wing, through which the consequences of things to come were obtained, must certainly have been directed by some excellent means to so noble an operation; for it is insufficient to attribute so great an effect to some natural ordinance, without the intelligence, agreement, or discourse of the agent which produces it; and such an opinion is evidently false." [Essays, ii. 12.]

Is it not a delightful thing to see a man who holds that nothing is either evidently true or evidently false, in a treatise expressly designed to establish Pyrrhonism, and to destroy evidence and certainty, deliver to us seriously these dreams as certain truths, and speak of the contrary opinion as evidently false? But he is amusing himself at our expense when he speaks in this way, and he is without excuse in thus sporting with his readers, by telling them things which he does not, and could not without absurdity, believe.

He was, without doubt, as good a philosopher as Virgil, who does not ascribe to any intelligence in the birds even those periodical changes which we observe in their movement according to the difference of the air, from which we may derive some conjecture as to rain and fine weather.

But these mistakes being voluntary, all that is necessary to avoid them is a little good faith. The most common, and the most dangerous, are those of which we are not conscious, because the engagement into which we have entered to defend an opinion disturbs the view of the mind, and leads it to take as true that which contributes to its end. The only remedy which can be applied to these is to have no end but truth, and to examine reasonings with so much care, that even prejudice shall not be able to mislead us.

CHAPTER III.

OF THE FALSE REASONINGS WHICH ARISE FROM OBJECTS THEMSELVES.

WE have already noticed that we ought not to separate the inward causes of our errors from those which are derived from objects, which may be called the outward, because the false appearance of these objects would not be capable of leading us into error, if the will did not hurry the mind into forming a precipitate judgment, when it is not as yet sufficiently enlightened.

Since, however, it cannot exert this power over the understanding in things perfectly evident, it is plain that the obscurity of the objects contributes somewhat to our mistakes; and, indeed, there are often cases in which the passion which leads us to reason ill is almost imperceptible. Hence it is useful to consider separately those illusions which arise principally from the things themselves:—

I.

It is a false and impious opinion, that truth is so like to falsehood, and virtue to vice, that it is impossible to distinguish between them; but it is true that, in the majority of cases, there is a mixture of truth and error, of virtue and vice, of perfection and imperfection, and that this mixture is one of the most ordinary sources of the false judgments of men.

For it is through this deceptive mixture that the good qualities of those whom we respect lead us to approve of their errors, and that the defects of those whom we do not esteem lead us to condemn what is good in them, since we do not consider that the most imperfect are not so in everything, and that God leaves in the best imperfections, which, being the remains of human infirmity, ought not to be the objects of our respect or imitation.

The reason of this is, that men rarely consider things in detail; they judge only according to their strongest impression, and perceive only what strikes them most; thus, when they perceive a good deal of truth in a discourse, they do not notice the errors which are mixed with it; and, on the contrary, when the truths are mingled with many errors, they pay attention only to the errors,—the strong bears away the weak, and the most vivid impression effaces that which is more obscure.

It is, however, a manifest injustice to judge in this way. There can be no possible reason for rejecting reason, and truth is not less truth for being mixed with error. It does not belong to men, although men may propound it. Thus, though men, by reason of their errors, may deserve to be condemned, the truth which they advance ought not to be rejected.

Thus justice and truth require, that in all things which are thus made up of good and evil we distinguish between them; and in this wise separation it is that mental precision mainly appears. Hence the fathers of the church have taken from pagan books very excellent things for their morals, and thus St. Augustine has not scrupled to borrow from a heretical Donatist seven rules for interpreting Scripture.

Reason obliges us, when we can, to make this distinction; but since we have not always time to examine in detail the good and evil that may be in everything, it is right, in such circumstances, to give to them the name which they deserve from their preponderating element. Thus we ought to say that a man is a good philosopher who commonly reasons well, and that a book is a good book which has notoriously more of good than of evil in it.

Men, however, are very much deceived in these general judgments; for they often praise and blame things from the consideration only of what is least important in them,—want of penetration leading them not to discover what is most important, when it is not the most striking: thus, although those who are wise judges in painting value infinitely more design than colour, or delicacy of touch, the ignorant are, nevertheless, more impressed by a painting whose colours are bright and vivid, than by another more sober in colour, however admirable in design.

It must, however, be confessed, that false judgments are not so common in the arts, since those who know nothing about them defer more readily to the opinion of those who are well informed; but they are most frequent in those things which lie within the jurisdiction of the people, and of which the world claims the liberty of judging, such as eloquence.

We call, for example, a preacher eloquent, when his periods are well turned, and when he uses no inelegant words; and from this M. Vaugelas says, in one place, that a bad word does a preacher or an advocate more harm than a bad reasoning. We must believe that this is simply a truth of fact which he relates, and not an opinion which he supports. It is true that we find people who judge in this way, but it is true also that there is nothing more unreasonable than these judgments; for the purity of language, and the multitude of figures, are but to eloquence what the colouring is to a painting—that is to say, only its lower and more sensuous part; but the most important part consists in conceiving things forcibly, and in expressing them so that we may convey to the minds of the hearers a bright and vivid image, which shall convey these things not only in an abstract form, but with the emotions also with which we conceive them; and this we may find in men of inelegant speech and unbalanced periods, while we meet with it rarely in those who pay so much attention to words and embellishments, since this care distracts their attention from things, and weakens the vigor of their thoughts,—as painters remark, that those who excel in colours do not commonly excel in design—the mind not being capable of this double application, and attention to the one injuring the other.

We may say, in general, that the world values most things by the exterior alone, since we find scarcely any who penetrate to the interior and to the foundation of them; everything is judged according to the fashion, and unhappy are those who are not in favour. Such a one is clever, intelligent, profound, as much as you will, but he does not speak fluently, and cannot turn a compliment well; he may reckon on being little esteemed through the whole of his life by the generality of the world, and on seeing a multitude of insignificant minds preferred before him. It is no great evil not to have the reputation which we merit, but it is a vast one to follow these false judgments, and to judge of things only superficially; and this we are bound, as far as possible, to avoid.

II.

Amongst the causes which lead us into error by a false lustre, which prevents our recognising it, we may justly reckon a certain grand and pompous eloquence, which Cicero calls *abundantem sonantibus verbis uberibusque setentiis;* for it is wonderful how sweetly a false reasoning flows in at the close of a period which well fits the ear, or of a figure which surprises us by its novelty, and in the contemplation of which we are delighted.

These ornaments not only veil from our view the falsehoods which mingle with discourse, but they insensibly engender them, since it often happens that they are necessary to the completion of the period or the figure. Thus, when we hear an orator commencing a long gradation, or an antithesis of many members, we have reason to be on our guard, since it rarely happens that he finishes without exaggerating the truth, in order to accommodate it to the figure. He commonly disposes of it as we do the stones of a building, or the metal of a statue : he cuts it, lengthens it, narrows it, disguises it, as he thinks fit, in order to adapt it to that vain work of words which he wishes to make.

How many false thoughts has the desire of making a good point produced! How many have been led into falsehood for the sake of a rhyme! How many foolish things have certain Italian authors been led to write, through the affectation of using only Ciceronian words, and of what is called pure Latinity! Who could help smiling to hear [Cardinal] Bembo say that a pope had been elected by the favour of the immortal gods—*Deorum immortalium beneficiis?* There are poets even who imagine that the essence of poetry consists in the introduction of pagan divinities; and a German poet, a good versifier enough, though not a very judicious writer, having been justly reproached by Francis Picus Mirandola with having introduced into a poem, where he describes the wars of Christians against Christians, all the divinities of paganism, and having mixed up Apollo, Diana, and Mercury, with the pope, the electors, and the emperor, distinctly maintained that, without this, it would not have been a poem,—in proof of which he alleged this strange reason, that the poems of Hesiod, of Homer, and of Virgil, are full of the names and the fables of these gods; whence he concluded that he might be allowed to do the same.

These bad reasonings are often imperceptible to those who make them, and deceive them first. They are deafened by the sound of their own words, dazzled with the lustre of their figures; and the grandeur of certain words attaches them unconsciously to thoughts of little solidity, which they would doubtless have rejected had they exercised a little reflection.

It is probable, for instance, that it was the word vestal which pleased an author of our time, and which led him to say to a young lady, to prevent her from being ashamed of knowing Latin, that she need not blush to speak a language which had been spoken by the vestals. For, if he had considered this thought, he would have seen that he might as justly have said to that lady that she ought to blush to speak a language which had been formerly spoken by the courtezans of Rome, who were far more numerous than the vestals; or that she ought to blush to speak any other language than that of her own country, since the ancient vestals spoke only their natural language. All these reasonings, which are worth nothing, are as good as that of this author;

and the truth is, that the vestals have nothing to do with justifying or condemning maidens who learn Latin.

The false reasonings of this kind, which are met with continually in the writings of those who most affect eloquence, show us how necessary it is for the majority of those who write or speak to be thoroughly convinced of this excellent rule,—*that there is nothing beautiful except that which is true;* which would take away from discourse a multitude of vain ornaments and false thoughts. It is true that this precision renders the style more dry and less pompous; but it also renders it clearer, more vigorous, more serious, and more worthy of an honourable man. The impression which it makes is less strong, but much more lasting; whereas that produced by these rounded periods is so transient, that it passes away almost as soon as we have heard them.

III.

It is a very common defect amongst men to judge rashly of the actions and intentions of others; and they almost always fall into it by a bad reasoning, through which, in not recognising with sufficient clearness all the causes which might produce any effect, they attribute that defect definitely to one cause, when it may have been produced by many others; or, again, suppose that a cause, which has accidentally, when united with many circumstances, produced an effect on one occasion, must do so on all occcasions.

A man of learning is found to be of the same opinion with a heretic, in a matter of criticism, independent of religious controversies: a malicious adversary concludes from this that he is favourable to heretics; but he concludes this rashly and maliciously, since it is perhaps reason and truth which have led him to adopt that opinion.

A writer may speak with some strength against an opinion which he believes to be dangerous; he will, from this, be accused of hatred and animosity against the authors who have advanced it; but he will be so unjustly and rashly, since this earnestness may arise from zeal for the truth, just as well as from hatred of the men who oppose it.

A man is the friend of a vicious man: it is, therefore, concluded that he is connected by some bond of interest with him, and is a partaker in his crimes. This does not follow: perhaps he knows nothing about them; and perhaps he has no part in them.

We fail to render true civility to those to whom it is due: we are said to be proud and insolent; but this was perhaps only an inadvertence or simple forgetfulness.

All exterior things are but equivocal signs, that is to say, signs which may signify many things; and we judge rashly when we determine this sign to mean a particular thing, without having any special reason for doing so. Silence is sometimes a sign of modesty and wisdom, and sometimes of stupidity. Slowness sometimes indicates prudence, and sometimes heaviness of mind. Change is sometimes a sign of inconstancy, and sometimes of sincerity. Thus it is bad reasoning to conclude that a man is inconstant, simply from the fact that he has changed his opinion; for he may have a good reason for changing it.

IV.

The false inductions by which general propositions are derived from some particular experiences, constitute one of the most common sources of the false reasonings of men. Three or four examples suffice them to make a *maxim* and a *common-place*, which they then employ as a principle fo deciding all things.

There are many maladies hidden from the most skilful physicians, and remedies often do not succeed: rash minds hence conclude that medicine is absolutely useless, and only a craft of charlatans.

There are light and loose women: this is sufficient for the jealous to conceive unjust suspicions against the most virtuous, and for licentious writers to condemn all universally.

There are some persons who hide great vices under an appearance of piety; libertines conclude from this that all devotion is no better than hypocrisy.

There are some things obscure and hidden, and we are often grossly deceived: all things are obscure and uncertain, say the ancient and modern Pyrrhonists, and we cannot know the truth of anything with certainty.

There is a want of equality in some of the actions of men, and this is enough to constitute a common-place, from which none are exempt. "Reason," say they, "is so weak and blind, that there is nothing so evidently clear as to be clear enough for it; the easy and the hard are both alike to it; all subjects are equal, and nature in general disclaims its jurisdiction. We only think what we *will* in the very moment in which we *will* it; we will nothing freely, nothing absolutely, nothing constantly."

Most people set forth the defects or good qualities of others only by general and extreme propositions. From some particular actions we infer a habit: from three or four faults we conclude a custom; and what happens once a month or once a year, happens every day, at every hour, and every moment, in the discourses of men,—so little pains do they take to observe in them the limits of truth and justice.

V.

It is a weakness and injustice which we often condemn, but which we rarely avoid, to judge of purposes by the event, and to reckon those who had taken a prudent resolution according to the circumstances, so far as they could see them, guilty of all the evil consequences which may have happened therefrom, either simply through accident, or through the malice of others who had thwarted it, or through some other circumstances which it was impossible for them to foresee.

Men not only love to be fortunate as much as to be wise, but they make no distinction between the fortunate and the wise, nor between the unfortunate and the guilty. This distinction is too subtile for them. We are ingenious in finding out the faults which we imagine have produced the want of success; and as astrologers, when they know a given event, fail not to discover the aspect of the stars which produced it, so also we never fail to find, after disgraces and misfortune, that those who have met with them have deserved them by some imprudence. He is unsuccessful, therefore he is in fault. In this way the world reasons, and in this way it has always reasoned, because there has always been little equity in the judgments of men, and because, not knowing the true causes of things, they substitute others according to the event, by praising those who are successful, and blaming those who are not.

VI.

But there are no false reasonings more common amongst men than those into which they fall, either by judging rashly of the truth of things from some authority insufficient to assure them of it, or by deciding the inward essence by the outward manner. We call the former the sophism of authority, the latter the sophism of the manner.

To understand how common these are, it is only necessary to consider that the majority of men are determined to believe one opinion rather than another, not by any solid and essential reasons which might lead them to know the truth, but by certain exterior and foreign marks which are more consonant to, or which they judge to be consonant to, truth, than to falsehood.

The reason of this is, that the interior truth of things is often deeply hidden; that the minds of men are commonly feeble and dark, full of clouds and false light, while their outward marks of truth are clear and sensible; so that, as men naturally incline to that which is easiest, they almost always range themselves on the side where they see those exterior marks of truth which are readily discovered.

These may be reduced to two principles,—the authority of him who propounds the thing, and the manner in which it is propounded. And these two ways of persuading are so powerful that they carry away almost all minds.

We may derive convincing arguments in matters of religion from the manner in which they are advanced. When we see, for example, in different ages of the church, and principally in the last, men who endeavour to propagate their opinions by bloodshed and the sword; when we see them arm themselves against the church by schism, against temporal powers by revolt; when we see people without the common commission, without miracles, without any external marks of piety, and with the plain marks rather of licentiousness, undertake to change the faith and discipline of the church in so criminal a manner, it is more than sufficient to make reasonable men reject them, and to prevent the most ignorant from listening to them.

But in those things, the knowledge of which is not absolutely necessary, and which God has left more to the discernment of the reason of each one in particular, the authority and the manner are not so important, and they often lead many to form judgments contrary to the truth.

We do not undertake to give here the rules and the precise limits of the respect which is due to authority in human things, we simply indicate some gross faults which are committed in this matter.

We often regard only the number of the witnesses, without at all considering whether the number increases the probability of their having discovered the truth, which is, however, unreasonable; for, as an author of our time has wisely remarked, in difficult things, which each must discover for himself, it is more likely that a single person will discover the truth than that many will. Thus the following is not a valid inference: this opinion is held by the majority of philosophers; it is, therefore, the truest.

We are often persuaded, by certain qualities which have no connection with the truth, of the things which we examine. Thus there are a number of people who trust implicitly to those who are older, and who have had more experience, even in those things which do not depend on age or experience, but on the clearness of the mind.

Piety, wisdom, moderation, are without doubt the most estimable qualities in the world, and they ought to give great authority to those who possess them in those things which depend on piety or sincerity, and even on the knowledge of God, for it is most probable that God communicates more to those who serve him more purely; but there are a multitude of things which depend only on human intelligence, human experience, and human penetration, and, in these things, those who have the superiority in intellect and in study, deserve to be relied on more than others. The contrary, however, often happens, and many reckon it best to follow, even in these things, the most devout men.

This arises, in part, from the fact that these advantages of mind are not so obvious as the external decorum which appears in pious persons, and in part, also, from the fact that men do not like to make these distinctions. Discrimination perplexes them; they will have all or nothing. If they trust to a man in one thing, they will trust to him in everything; if they do not in one, they will not in any; they love short, plain, and easy ways. But this disposition, though common, is nevertheless contrary to reason, which shows us that the same persons are not to be trusted to in anything, because they are not distinguished in anything; and that it is bad reasoning to conclude: he is a serious man, therefore he is intelligent and clever in everything.

VII.

It is true, indeed, that if any errors are pardonable, those into which we fall through our excessive deference to the opinion of good men are among the number. But there is a delusion much more absurd in itself, but which is nevertheless very common, that, namely, of believing that a man speaks the truth because he is a man of birth, of fortune, or high in office.

Not that any formally make these kinds of reasonings—he has a hundred thousand livres a year; therefore he possesses judgment: he is of high birth; therefore what he advances must be true: he is a poor man; therefore he is wrong. Nevertheless, something of this kind passes through the minds of the majority, and unconsciously bears away their judgment.

Let the same thing be proposed by a man of quality, and by one of no distinction, and it will often be found that we approve of it in the mouth of the former, when we scarcely condescend to listen to it in that of the latter. Scripture designed to teach us this disposition of men, in that perfect representation which is given of it in the book of Ecclesiasticus.* "When a rich man speaketh, every one holdeth his tongue, and look, what he saith they extol it to the skies ; but if the poor man speak, they say, ' What fellow is this ?' " *(Dives locutus est, et omnes tacuerunt, et verbum illius usque ad nubes perducent; pauper locutus est, et dicunt, Quis est hic ?)*

It is certain that complaisance and flattery have much to do with the approbation which is bestowed on the actions and words of people of quality ; as also that they often gain this by a certain outward grace, and by a noble, free, and natural bearing, which is sometimes so distinctive that it is almost impossible for it to be imitated by those who are of low birth. It is certain, also, that there are many who approve of everything which is done and said by the great, through an inward abasement of soul, who bend under the weight of grandeur, and whose sight is not strong enough to bear its lustre ; as, indeed, that the outward pomp which environs them always imposes a little, and makes some impression on the strongest minds.

This illusion springs from the corruption of the heart of man, who, having a strong passion for honours and pleasures,

---

* Ecclesiasticus xiii. 23.

necessarily conceives a great affection for the means by which these honours and pleasures are obtained. The love which we have for all those things which are valued by the world, makes us judge those happy who possess them; and, in thus judging them happy, we place them above ourselves, and regard them as eminent and exalted persons. This habit of regarding them with respect passes insensibly from their fortune to their mind. Men do not commonly do things by halves: we, therefore, give them minds as exalted as their rank; we submit to their opinions; and this is the reason of the credit which they commonly obtain in the affairs which they manage.

But this illusion is still stronger in the great themselves, when they have not laboured to correct the impression which their fortune naturally makes on their minds, than it is in their inferiors. Some derive from their estate and riches a reason for maintaining that their opinions ought to prevail over those who are beneath them. They cannot bear that those people whom they regard with contempt should pretend to have as much judgment and reason as themselves, and this makes them so impatient of the least contradiction. All this springs from the same source, that is, from the false ideas which they have of their grandeur, nobility, and wealth. Instead of considering them as things altogether foreign from their character, which do not prevent them at all from being perfectly equal to all the rest of men, both in mind and body, and which do not prevent their judgment even from being as weak and as liable to be deceived as that of all others, they, in some sort, incorporate with their very essence all these qualities of grand, noble, rich, master, lord, prince,—they exaggerate their idea of themselves with these things, and never represent themselves to themselves without all their titles, their equipage, and their train.

They are accustomed from their infancy to consider themselves as of a different species from other men; they never mingle in imagination with the mass of human kind; they are, in their own eyes, always counts or dukes, and never simply men. Thus they shape to themselves a soul and judgment according to the measure of their fortune, and believe themselves as much above others in mind as they are above them in birth and fortune.

The folly of the human mind is such, that there is nothing which may not serve to aggrandise the idea which it has of itself. A beautiful horse, grand clothes, a long beard, make men consider themselves more clever; and there are few who do not think more of themselves on horseback or in a coach than on foot. It is easy to convince everybody that there is nothing more ridiculous than these judgments, but it is very difficult to guard entirely against the secret impression which these outward things make upon the mind. All that we can do is to accustom ourselves as much as possible to give no influence at all to those qualities which cannot contribute towards finding the truth, and to give it even to those which do thus contribute only so far as they really contribute to this end. Age, knowledge, study, experience, mind, energy, memory, accuracy, labour, avail to find the truth of hidden things, and these qualities, therefore, deserve to be respected; but it is always necessary to weigh with care, and then to make a comparison with the opposite reasons; for from separate individual things we can conclude nothing with certainty, since there are very false opinions which have been sanctioned by men of great mental power, who possessed these qualities to a great extent.

VIII.

There is something still more deceptive in the mistakes which arise from the manner, for we are naturally led to believe that a man is in the right when he speaks with grace, with ease, with gravity, with moderation, and with gentleness; and, on the contrary, that a man is in the wrong when he speaks harshly, or manifests anything of passion, acrimony, or presumption, in his actions and words.

Nevertheless, if we judge of the essence of things by these outward and sensible appearances, we must be often deceived. For there are many people who utter follies gravely and modestly; and others, on the contrary, who, being naturally of a quick temper, or under the influence even of some passion, which appears in their countenance or their words, have nevertheless the truth on their side. There are some men of very moderate capacity, and very superficial, who, from having been nourished at court, where the art of pleasing is studied and practised better than anywhere else, have very agreeable manners, by means of which they render many false judgments acceptable; and there are others, on the contrary, who, having nothing outward to recommend them, have, nevertheless, a great and solid mind within. There are some who speak better than they think, and others who think better than they speak. Thus reason demands of those who are capable of it, that they judge not by these outward things, and hesitate not to yield to the truth, not only when it is proposed in ways that are offensive and disagreeable, but even when it is mingled with much of falsehood; for the same person may speak truly in one thing, and falsely in another; may be right in one thing, and wrong in another.

It is necessary, therefore, to consider each thing separately, that is to say, we must judge of the manner by the manner, and of the matter by the matter, and not of the matter by the manner, nor of the manner by the matter. A man does wrong to speak with anger, and he does right to speak the truth; and, on the contrary, another is right in speaking calmly and civilly, and he is wrong in advancing falsehoods.

But as it is reasonable to be on our guard against concluding that a thing is true or false, because it is proposed in such a way, it is right, also, that those who wish to persuade others of any truth which they have discovered, should study to clothe it in the garb most suitable for making it acceptable, and to avoid those revolting ways of stating it which only lead to its rejection.

They ought to remember that when we seek to move the minds of people, it is a small thing that we have right on our side; and it is a great evil to have only right, and not to have also that which is necessary for making it acceptable.

If they seriously honour the truth, they ought not to dishonour it by covering it with the marks of falsehood and deceit; and if they love it sincerely, they ought not to attach to it the hatred and aversion of men, by the offensive way in which they propound it. It is the most important, as well as the most useful precept of rhetoric, that it behoves us to govern the spirit as well as the words; for although it is a different thing to be wrong in the manner from being wrong in the matter, the faults, nevertheless, of the manner are often greater and more important than those of the matter.

In reality, all these fiery, presumptuous, bitter, obstinate, passionate manners, always spring from some disorder of the mind, which is often more serious than the defect of intelligence and of knowledge, which we reprehend in others. It is, indeed, always unjust to seek to persuade men in this way; for it is very right that we should lead them to the truth when we know it; but it is wrong to compel others to take as true everything that we believe, and to defer to our authority alone. We do this, however, when we propose the truth in this offensive manner. For the way of speaking generally enters into the mind before the reasons, since the mind is more prompt to notice the manner of the speaker than it is to comprehend the solidity of his proofs, which are often, indeed, not comprehended at all. Now the manner of the discourse being thus separated from the proofs, marks only the authority which he who speaks arrogates to himself; so that if he is bitter and imperious, he necessarily revolts the minds of others, since he appears to wish to gain, by authority, and by a kind of tyranny, that which ought only to be obtained by persuasion and reason.

This injustice is still greater when we employ these offensive ways in combating common and received opinions; for the judgment of an individual may indeed be preferred to that of many when it is more correct, but an individual ought never to maintain that his authority should prevail against that of all others.

Thus, not only modesty and prudence, but justice itself, obliges us to assume a modest air when we combat common opinions or established authority, otherwise we cannot escape the injustice of opposing the authority of an individual to an authority either public, or greater and more widely established than our own. We cannot exercise too much modern-tion when we seek to disturb the position of a received opinion or of an ancient faith. This is so true, that St. Augustine extended it even to religious truths, having given this excellent rule to all those who have to instruct others:—

"Observe," says he, "in what way the wise and religious catholics taught that which they had to communicate to others. If they were things common and authorized, they propounded them in a manner full of assurance, and free from every trace of doubt by being accompanied with the greatest possible gentleness; but if they were extraordinary things, although they themselves very clearly recognized their truth, they still proposed them rather as *doubts* and as *questions* to be examined, than as dogmas and fixed decisions, in order to accommodate themselves in this to the weakness of those who heard them." And so if a truth be so high that it is above the strength of those to whom it is spoken, they prefer rather to keep it back for a while, in order to give them time for growth, and for becoming capable of receiving it, instead of making it known to them that state of weakness in which it would have overwhelmed them.

LECTURES

OF

SIR WILLIAM HAMILTON

ON

MODIFIED LOGIC.

LECTURES ON LOGIC.

LECTURE I.—MODIFIED LOGIC.

PART I.—MODIFIED STOICHEIOLOGY.

SECTION I.—DOCTRINE OF TRUTH AND ERROR.

TRUTH—ITS CHARACTER AND KINDS.

HAVING now terminated the Doctrine of Pure or Abstract Logic, we proceed to that of Modified or Concrete Logic. In entering on this subject, I have to recall to your memory what has formerly been stated in regard to the object which Modified Logic proposes for consideration. Pure Logic takes into account only the necessary conditions of thought, as founded on the nature of the thinking process itself. Modified Logic, on the contrary, considers the conditions to which thought is subject, arising from the empirical circumstances, external and internal, under which exclusively it is the will of our Creator that man should manifest his faculty of thinking. Pure Logic is thus exclusively conversant with the form; Modified Logic is, likewise, occupied with the matter, of thought. And as their objects are different,

[margin: Modified Logic,—its object]

so, likewise, must be their ends. The end of Pure Logic is formal truth,—the harmony of thought with thought; the end of Modified Logic is the harmony of thought with existence. Of these ends, that which Pure Logic proposes is less ambitious, but it is fully and certainly accomplished; the end which Modified Logic proposes is higher, but it is far less perfectly attained. The problems which Modified Logic has to solve may be reduced to three:

Its problems,—reduced to three. 1°, What is truth and its contradictory opposite,—Error? 2°, What are the Causes of Error, and the Impediments to Truth, by which man is beset in the employment of his faculties, and what are the Means of their Removal? And, 3°, What are the Subsidiaries by which Human Thought may be strengthened and guided in the exercise of its functions?

From this statement it is evident that Concrete Logic might, like Pure Logic, have been divided into a Stoicheiology and a Methodology,—

And distributed between its Stoicheiology and its Methodology. the former comprising the first two heads, —the latter the third. For if to Modified Stoicheiology we refer the consideration of the nature of concrete truth and error, and of the conditions of a merely not erroneous employment of thought,—this will be exausted in the First and Second Chapters; whereas, if we refer to Methodology a consideration of the means of employing thought not merely without error, but with a certain positive perfection,—this is what the Third Chapter professes to expound.

I commence the First Chapter, which proposes to answer the question,—What is Truth? with its correlatives,—by the dictation of the following paragraphs:

¶ I. The end which all our scientific efforts are exerted to accomplish, is *Truth* and *Certainty*. Truth is the correspondence or agreement of a cognition with its object; its Criterion is the necessity determined by the laws which govern our faculties of knowledge; and Certainty is the consciousness of this necessity. Certainty, or the conscious necessity of knowledge, absolutely excludes the admission of any opposite supposition. Where such appears admissible, doubt and uncertainty arise. If we consider truth by relation to the degree and kind of Certainty, we have to distinguish *Knowledge, Belief,* and *Opinion.* Knowledge and Belief differ not only in degree, but in kind. Knowledge is a certainty founded upon insight; Belief is a certainty founded upon feeling. The one is perspicuous and objective; the other is obscure and subjective. Each, however, supposes the other; and an assurance is said to be a knowledge or a belief, according as the one element or the other preponderates. Opinion is the admission of something as true, where, however, neither insight nor feeling is so intense as to necessitate a perfect certainty. What prevents the admission of a proposition as certain is called *Doubt.* The approximation of the imperfect certainty of opinion to the perfect certainty of knowledge or belief is called *Probability.*

Par. I. Truth and Certainty,—what.

If we consider Truth with reference to Knowledge, and to the way in which this knowledge arises, we must distinguish *Empirical* or *a posteriori,* from *Pure* or *a priori Truth.* The former has reference to cognitions which have their source in the presentations of

Perception, External and Internal, and which obtain their form by the elaboration of the Understanding or faculty of Relations (διάνοια). The latter is contained in the necessary and universal cognitions afforded by the Regulative Faculty—Intellect Proper—or Common Sense (νοῦς).

This paragraph, after stating that Truth and Certainty constitute the end of all our endeavors after knowledge, for only in the attainment of truth and certainty can we possibly attain to knowledge or science;—I say, after the statement of this manifest proposition,—it proceeds to define what is meant by the two terms *Truth* and *Certainty;* and, to commence with the former,—Truth is defined, the correspondence or agreement of a cognition or cofinitive act of thought with its object.

Explication.

The question—What is truth? is an old and celebrated problem. It was proposed by the Roman Governor—by Pontius Pilate—to our Saviour; and it is a question which still recurs, and is still keenly agitated in the most recent schools of Philosophy. In one respect all are nearly agreed in regard to the definition of the term, for all admit that by truth is understood a harmony,—an agreement, a correspondence between our thought and that which we think about. This definition of truth we owe to the schoolmen. "*Veritas intellectus,*" says Acquinas, "*est adæquatio intellectus et rei, secundum quod intellectus dicit esse, quod est, vel non esse, qoud non est.*" From the schoolmen, this definition has been handed down to modern philosophers, by whom it is currently employed, without, in general, a suspicion of its origin. It is not, therefore, in regard to the meaning of the term *truth*, that there is any

Truth,—what.

Definition of the term.

difference of opinion among philosophers. The questions which have provoked discussion, and which remain, as heretofore, without a definitive solution, are not whether truth be the harmony of thought and reality, but whether this harmony, or truth, be attainable, and whether we possess any criterion by which we can be assured of its attainment. Considering, however, at present only the meaning of the term, philosophers have divided the Truth (or the harmony of thought and its object) into different species, to which they have given diverse names; but they are at one neither in the division nor in the nomenclature.

Questions in debate regarding Truth.

It is plain that for man there can only be conceived two kinds of truth, because there are for human thought only two species of object. For that about which we think must either be a thought, or something which a thought contains. On this is founded the distinction of Formal Knowledge and Real Knowledge,—of Formal Truth and Real Truth. Of these in their order:

For man only two kinds of Truth,—Formal and Real.

I. In regard to the former, a thought abstracted from what it contains, that is, from its matter or what it is conversant about, is the more form of thought. The knowledge of the form of thought is a formal knowledge, and the harmony of thought with the form of thought is, consequently, Formal Truth. Now Formal Knowledge is of two kinds; for it regards either the conditions of the Elaborative Faculty,—the Faculty of Thought Proper,—or the conditions of our Presentations or Representations of external things, that is, the intuitions of Space and Time. The former of these sciences is Pure

I. Formal Truth.

Formal Truth of two kinds,—Logical and Mathematical.

4*

Logic—the science which considers the laws to which the Understanding is astricted in its elaborative operations, without enquiring what is the object,—what is the matter, to which these operations are applied. The latter of these sciences is Mathematics, or the science of Quantity, which considers the relations of Time and Space, without enquiring whether there be any actual reality in space or time. Formal truth will, therefore, be of two kinds,—Logical and Mathematical. Logical truth is the harmony or agreement of our thoughts with themselves as thoughts, in other words, the correspondence of thought with the universal laws of thinking. These laws are the object of Pure or General Logic, and in these it places the criterion of truth. This criterion is, however, only the negative condition—only the *conditio sine qua non*, of truth. Logical truth is supposed in supposing the possibility of thought; for all thought presents a combination, the elements of which are repugnant or congruent, but which cannot be repugnant and congruent at the same time. Logic might be true, although we possessed no truth beyond its fundamental laws; although we knew nothing of any real existence beyond the formal hypothesis of its possibility.

Logical Truth.

But were the Laws of Logic purely subjective, that is, were they true only for our thought alone, and without any objective validity, all human sciences (and Mathematics among the rest) would be purely subjective likewise; for we are cognizant of objects only under the forms and rules of which Logic is the scientific development. If the true character of objective validity be universality, the Laws of Logic are really of that character, for these laws constrain

TRUTH—ITS CHARACTER AND KINDS. 59

us, by their own authority, to regard them as the universal laws not only of human thought, but of universal reason.

The case is the same with the other formal science, the science of Quantity, or Mathematics. Without inquiring into the reality of existences, and without borrowing from, or attributing to, them anything, Arithmetic, the science of Discrete Quantity, creates its numbers, and Geometry, the science of Continuous Quantity, creates its figures; and both operate upon these their objects in absolute independence of all external actuality. The two mathematical sciences are dependent for their several objects only on the notion of time and the notion of space,—notions under which alone matter can be conceived as possible, for all matter supposes space, and all matter is moved in space and time. But to the notions of space and time the existence or non-existence of matter is indifferent; indifferent, consequently, to Geometry and Arithmetic, so long at least as they remain in the lofty regions of pure speculation, and do not descend to the practical application of their principles. If matter had no existence, nay, if space and time existed only in our minds, mathematics would still be true; but their truth would be of a purely formal and ideal character,—would furnish us with no knowledge of objective realities.

Mathematical Truth.

So much for Formal Truth, under its two species of Logical and Mathematical.

The other genus of truth—(the end which the Real Sciences propose)—is the harmony between a thought and its matter. The Real Sciences are those which have a determinate reality for their object, and which are conversant about existences other than the forms of thought.

II. Real Truth.
Real and Formal Sciences.

The Formal Sciences have a superior certainty to the real; for they are simply ideal combinations, and they construct their objects without inquiring about their objective reality. The real sciences are sciences of fact, for the point from which they depart is always a fact,— always a presentation. Some of these rest on the presentations of Self-consciousness, or the facts of mind; others on the presentations of Sensitive Perception, or the facts of nature. The former are the Mental Sciences, the latter the Material. The facts of mind are given partly as contingent, partly as necessary; the latter—the necessary facts—are universal virtually and in themselves; the former—the contingent facts—only obtain a fictitious universality by a process of generalization. The facts of nature, however necessary in themselves, are given to us only as contingent and isolated phænomena; they have, therefore, only that conditional, that empirical, generality, which we bestow on them by classification.

<small>Under the Real Sciences are included the Mental and Material.</small>

Real truth is, therefore, the correspondence of our thoughts with the existences which constitute their objects. But here a difficulty arises:—How can we know that there is, that there can be, such a correspondence? All that we know of the objects is through the presentations of our faculties; but whether these present the objects as they are in themselves, we can never ascertain, for to do this it would be requisite to go out of ourselves,—out of our faculties,—to obtain a knowledge of the objects by other faculties, and thus to compare our old presentations with our new. But all this, even were the supposition possible, would be incompetent to

<small>How can we know that there is a correspondence between our thought and its object?</small>

afford us the certainty required. For were it possible to leave our old, and to obtain a new, set of faculties, by which to test the old, still the veracity of these new faculties would be equally obnoxious to doubt as the veracity of the old. For what guarantee could we obtain for the credibility in the one case, which we do not already possess in the other? The new faculties could only assert their own truth; but this is done by the old; and it is impossible to imagine any presentations of the non-ego by any finite intelligence, to which a doubt might not be raised, whether these presentations were not merely subjective modifications of the conscious ego itself. All that could be said in answer to such a doubt is, that if such were true, our whole nature is a lie,—a supposition which is not, without the strongest evidence, to be admitted; and the argument is as competent against the sceptic in our present condition, as it would be were we endowed with any other conceivable form of Acquisitive and Cognitive Faculties. But I am here trenching on what ought to be reserved for an explanation of the Criterion of Truth.

Such, as it appears to me, is the only rational division of Truth according to the different character of the objects to which thought is relative, —into Formal and into Real Truth. Formal Truth, as we have seen, is subdivided into Logical and into Mathematical. Real Truth might likewise be subdivided, were this requisite, into various species. For example, Metaphysical Truth might denote the harmony of thought with the necessary facts of mind; Psychological Truth, the harmony of thought with the contingent facts of mind; and Physical Truth, the harmony of thought with the phænomena of external experience.

Real Truth,—its subdivisions.

Metaphysical. Psychological. Physical.

It now remains to say a word in regard to the confusion which has been introduced into this subject, by the groundless distinctions and contradictions of philosophers. Some have absurdly given the name of *truth* to the mere reality of existence, altogether abstracted from any conception or judgment relative to it, in any intelligence, human or divine. In this sense *physical truth* has been used to denote the actual existence of a thing. Some have given the name of *metaphysical truth* to the congruence of the thing with its idea in the mind of the Creator. Others again have bestowed the name of *metaphysical truth* on the mere logical possibility of being thought; while they have denominated by *logical truth* the metaphysical or physical correspondence of thought with its objects. Finally, the term *moral* or *ethical truth* has been given to veracity, or the correspondence of thought with its expression. In this last case, truth is not, as in the others, employed in relation to thought and its object, but to thought and its enouncement. So much for the notion, and the principal distinctions of Truth.

<small>Various applications of the term *Truth*.</small>

But, returning to the paragraph; I take the next clause, which is,—"The Criterion of truth is the necessity determined by the laws which govern our faculties of knowledge; and the consciousness of this necessity is certainty." That the necessity of a cognition, that is, the impossibility of thinking it other than as it is presented,—that this necessity, as founded on the laws of thought, is the criterion of truth, is shown by the circumstance that where such necessity is found, all doubt in regard to the correspondence of the cognitive thought and its object must vanish; for to doubt

<small>The Criterion of Truth.</small>

whether what we necessarily think in a certain manner, actually exists as we conceive it, is nothing less than an endeavor to think the necessary as the not necessary or the impossible, which is contradictory.

What has just been said also illustrates the truth of the next sentence of the paragraph, viz.,—" Certainty or the conscious necessity of a cognition absolutely excludes the admission of any opposite supposition. When such is found to be admissible, doubt and uncertainty arise." This sentence requiring no explanation, I proceed to the next, viz., —" If we consider truth by the relation to the degree and kind of Certainty, we have to distinguish Knowledge, Belief, and Opinion. Knowledge and Belief differ not only in degree but in kind. Knowledge is a certainty founded on intuition. Belief is a certainty founded upon feeling. The one is perspicuous and objective, the other is obscure and subjective. Each, however, supposes the other, and an assurance is said to be a knowledge or a belief, according as the one element or the other preponderates."

In reference to this passage, it is necessary to say something in regard to the difference of Knowledge and Belief. In common language the word *Belief* is often used to denote an inferior degree of certainty. We may, however, be equally certain of what we believe as of what we know, and it has, not without ground, been maintained by many philosophers, both in ancient and in modern times, that the certainty of all knowledge is, in its ultimate analysis, resolved into a certainty of belief. "All things," says Luther, "stand in a belief, in a faith, which he can neither see nor comprehend. The

<small>Knowledge and Belief—their difference.</small>

<small>That the certainty of all knowledge is ultimately resolvable into a certainty of Belief, maintained by Luther.</small>

man who would make these visible, manifest, and comprehensible, has vexation and heart-grief for his reward. May the Lord increase Belief in you and in others." But you may perhaps think that the saying of Luther is to be taken theologically, and that, philosophically considered, all belief ought to be founded on knowledge, not all knowledge in belief. But the same doctrine is held even by those philosophers who are the least disposed to mysticism or blind faith. Among these Aristotle stands distinguished. He defines science, strictly so called, or the knowledge of indubitable truths,. merely by the intensity of our conviction or subjective assurance ; and on a primary and incomprehensible belief he hangs the whole chain of our comprehensible or immediate knowledge. The doctrine which has been called *The Philosophy of Common Sense,* is the doctrine which founds all our knowledge on belief; and, though this has not been signalized, the doctrine of Common Sense is perhaps better stated by the Stagirite than by any succeeding thinker. "What," he says, "appears to all men, that we affirm to be, and he who rejects this belief (πίστις) will assuredly advance nothing better worthy of credit." This passage is from his *Nicomachean Ethics.* But, in his Physical Treatises, he founds in belief the knowledge we have of the reality of motion, and by this, as a source of knowledge paramount to the Understanding, he supersedes the contradictions which are involved in our conception of motion, and which had so acutely been evolved by the Eleatic Zeno, in order to show that motion was impossible. In like manner, in his Logical Treatises, Aristotle shows that the primary or ultimate principles of knowledge must be incomprehensible ; for if comprehensible, they must be comprehended in some higher

[margin: Aristotle.]

notion, and this again, if not itself incomprehensible, must be again comprehended in a still higher, and so on in a progress *ad infinitum,* which is absurd. But what is given as an ultimate and incomprehensible principle of knowledge, is given as a fact, the existence of which we must admit, but the reasons of whose existence we cannot know,—we cannot understand. But such an admission, as it is not a knowledge, must be a belief; and thus it is that, according to Aristotle, all our knowledge is in its root a blind, a passive faith, in other words, a feeling. The same doctrine was subsequently held by many of the acutest thinkers of ancient times, more especially among the Platonists; and of these Proclus is perhaps the philosopher in whose works the doctrine is turned to the best account. In modern times we may trace it in silent operation, though not explicitly proclaimed, or placed as the foundation of a system. It is found spontaneously recognized even by those who might be supposed the least likely to acknowledge it without compulsion. Hume, for example, against whose philosophy the doctrine of Common Sense was systematically arrayed, himself pointed out the weapons by which his adversaries subsequently assailed his scepticism; for he himself was possessed of too much philosophical acuteness not to perceive that the root of knowledge is belief. Thus, in his *Inquiry,* he says,—" It seems evident that men are carried by a natural instinct or prepossession to repose faith in their senses: and that, without any reasoning, or even almost before the use of reason, we always suppose an external universe which depends not on our preception, but would exist though we and every sensible creature were absent or annihilated. Even the animal

[margin: The Platonists. Proclus.]
[margin: Hume.]

creation are governed by a like opinion, and preserve this belief,—the belief of external objects, in all their thoughts, designs, and actions. . . . . This very table which we see white, and which we feel hard, is believed to exist independent of our perception, and to be something external to our mind which perceives it."

But, on the other hand, the manifestation of this belief necessarily involves knowledge; for we cannot believe without some consciousness or knowledge of the belief, and, consequently, without some consciousnesss or knowledge of the object of the belief. Now the immediate consciousness or knowledge of an object is called an *intuition*,—an *insight*. It is thus impossible to separate belief and knowledge,—feeling and intuition. They each suppose the other.

<small>The manifestation of Belief involves Knowledge.</small>

<small>Intuition,—what.</small>

The consideration, however, of the relation of Belief and Knowledge does not properly belong to Logic, except in so far as it is necessary to explain the nature of Truth and Error. It is altogether a metaphysical discussion; and one of the most difficult problems of which Metaphysics attempts the solution.

<small>The question as to the relation of Belief and Knowledge properly metaphysical.</small>

The remainder of the paragraph contains the statement of certain distinctions and the definition of certain terms, which it was necessary to signalize, but which do not require any commentary for their illustration. The only part that might have required an explanation is the distinction of Truth into Pure, or *a priori*, and into Empirical, or *a posteriori*. The explanation of this division has been already given more than once, but the following may now be added.

Experience presents to us only individual objects, and as these individual objects might or might not have come within our sphere of observation, our whole knowledge of and from these objects might or might not exist;—it is merely accidental or contingent. But as our knowledge of individual objects affords the possibility, as supplying the whole contents, of our generalized or abstracted notions, our generalized or abstracted notions are, consequently, not more necessary to thought, than the particular observations out of which they are constructed. For example, every horse I have seen I might not have seen; and I feel no more necessity to think the reality of a horse than the reality of a hippogriff; I can, therefore, easily annihilate in thought the existence of the whole species. I can suppose it not to be,—not to have been. The case is the same with every other notion which is mediately or immediately the datum of observation. We can think away each and every part of the knowledge we have derived from experience; our whole empirical knowledge is, therefore, a merely accidental possession of the mind.

Pure and Empirical Truth.

But there are notions in the mind of a very different character,—notions which we cannot but think, if we think at all. These, therefore, are notions necessary to the mind; and, as necessary, they cannot be the product of experience. For example, I perceive something to begin to be. I feel no necessity to think that this thing must be at all, but thinking it existent, I cannot but think that it has a cause. The notion, or rather the judgment, of Cause and Effect, is, therefore, necessary to the mind. If so, it cannot be derived from experience.

LECTURE II.—MODIFIED STOICHEIOLOGY.

SECTION I.—DOCTRINE OF TRUTH AND ERROR.

SECTION II.—ERROR,—ITS CAUSES AND REMEDIES.

A.—GENERAL CIRCUMSTANCES—SOCIETY.

I NOW proceed to the consideration of the opposite of Truth,—Error, and, on this subject, give you the following paragraph:

¶ II. Error is opposed to Truth; and Error arises, 1°, From the commutation of what is Subjective and what is Objective in thought; 2°, From the Contradiction of a supposed knowledge with its Laws; or, 3°, From a want of Adequate Activity in our Cognitive Faculties.

Par. II. Error,—its character and sources.

Error is to be discriminated from *Ignorance* and from *Illusion;* these, however, along with Arbitrary Assumption, afford the most frequent occasions of error.

This paragraph consists of two parts, and these I shall successively consider. The first is: "Error is opposed to truth; and Error arises,— 1°, From the commutation of what is subjective with what is objective in thought; 2°, From the contradiction of a

Explication.

supposed knowledge with its laws ; or, 3°, From a want of adequate activity in our cognitive faculties."

"In the first place, we have seen that Truth is the agreement of a thought with its object. Now, as Error is the opposite of truth,—Error must necessarily consist in a want of this agreement. In the second place, it has been shown that the criterion or standard of truth is the necessity founded on the laws of our cognitive faculties ; and from this it follows that the essential character of error must be, either that it is not founded on these laws, or that it is repugnant to them. But these two alternatives may be viewed as only one ; for inasmuch as, in the former case, the judgment remains undecided, and can make no pretence to certainty, it may be thrown out of account no less than in the latter, where, as positively contradictory of the laws of knowledge, it is necessarily false. Of these statements the first, that is, the non-agreement of a notion with its object, is error viewed on its material side ; and as a notion is the common product,—the joint result afforded by the reciprocal action of object and subject,·it is evident that whatever the notion contains not correspondent to the object, must be a contribution by the thinking subject alone, and we are thus warranted in saying that Material Error consists in the commuting of what is subjective with what is objective in thought ; in other words, in mistaking an ideal illusion for a real representation. The second of these statements, that is, the incongruence of the supposed cognition with the laws of knowledge, is error viewed on its formal side. Now here the question at once presents itself,—How can an act of

Error,—what.

As Material.

As Formal.

cognition contradict its own laws? The answer is that it cannot; and error, when more closely scrutinized, is found not so much to consist in the contradictory activity of our cognitive faculties as in their want of activity. And this may be in consequence of one or other of two causes. For it may arise from some other mental power,—the will, for example, superseding,—taking the place of, the defective cognition, or, by its intenser force, turning it aside and leading it to a false result; or it may arise from some want of relative perfection in the object, so that the cognitive faculty is not determined by it to the requisite degree of action.

Arises from the want of adequate activity of the Cognitive Faculties.

"What is actually thought, cannot but be correctly thought. Error first commences when thinking is remitted, and can in fact only gain admission in virtue of the truth which it contains;—every error is a perverted truth. Hence Descartes is justified in the establishment of the principle,—that we would never admit the false for the true, if we would only give assent to what we clearly and distinctly apprehend. · ' *Nihil nos unquam falsum pro vero admissuros, si tantum iis assensum præbeamus, quæ clare et distincte percipimus.*'" In this view the saying of the Roman poet—

"*Nam neque decipitur ratio, nec decipit unquam,*"

—is no longer a paradox; for the condition of error is not the activity of intelligence, but its inactivity.

So much for the first part of the paragraph. The second is—"Error is to be discriminated from Ignorance and from Illusion, which, however, along with Arbitrary Assumption, afford the usual occasions of Error."

Error discriminated from Ignorance and Illusion.

"Ignorance is a mere negation,—a mere not-knowledge;
whereas in error there lies a positive pretence to knowledge. Hence a representa-
tion, be it imperfect, be it even without any correspondent
objective reality, is not in itself an error. The imagination of a hippogriff is not in itself false; the Orlando
Furioso is not a tissue of errors. Error only arises when
we attribute to the creations of our minds some real
object, by an assertory judgment; we do not err and deceive
either ourselves or others, when we hold and enounce a subjective or problematic supposition only for what it is.
Ignorance,—not knowledge,—however, leads to error, when
we either regard the unknown as non-existent, or when we
falsely fill it up. The latter is, however, as much the result
of Will, of arbitrary assumption, as of ignorance; and,
frequently, it is the result of both together. In general,
the will has no inconsiderable share in the activity by which
knowledge is realized. The will has not immediately an
influence on our judgment, but mediately it has. Attention
is an act of volition, and attention furnishes to the understanding the elements of its decision. The will determines
whether we shall carry on our investigations, or break them
off, content with the first apparent probability; and whether
we shall apply our observations to all, or, only partially, to
certain, momenta of determination.

"The occasions of Error which lie in those qualities of
Presentation, Representation, and Thought
Illusion.
arising from the conditions and influences
of the thinking subject itself, are called *Illusions*. But the
existence of illusion does not necessarily imply the existence
of error. Illusion becomes error only when we attribute to
it objective truth; whereas illusion is no error when we

regard the fallacious appearance as a mere subjective affection. In the jaundice, we see everything tinged with yellow, in consequence of the suffusion of the eye with bile. In this case, the yellow vision is illusion; and it would become error, were we to suppose that the objects we perceive were really so colored. All the powers which co-operate to the formation of our judgments may become the sources of illusion, and, consequently, the occasions of error. The Senses, the Presentative Faculties, External and Internal, the Representative, the Retentive, the Reproductive, and the Elaborative Faculties, are immediate, the Feelings and the Desires are mediate, sources of illusion. To these must be added the Faculty of Signs, in all its actual manifestations in language. Hence we speak of sensible, psychological, moral, and symbolical, illusion. In all these relations the causes of illusion are partly general, partly particular; and though they proximately manifest themselves in some one or other of these forms, they may ultimately be found contained in the circumstances by which the mental character of the individual is conformed. Taking, therefore, a general view of all the possible Sources of Error, I think they may be reduced to the following classes, which, as they constitute the heads and determine the order of the ensuing discussion, I shall comprise in the following paragraph, with which commences the consideration of the Second Chapter of Modified Logic. Before, however, proceeding to consider these several classes in their order, I may observe that Bacon is the first philosopher who attempted a systematic enumeration of the various sources of error; and his quaint classification of these, under the significant name of *idols*, into the

<small>Its sources.</small>

<small>Bacon's classification of the sources of error.</small>

four genera of Idols of the Tribe (*idola tribus*), Idols of the Den (*idola specus*), Idols of the Forum (*idola fori*), which may mean either the market-place, the bar, or the place of public assembly, and Idols of the Theatre (*idola theatri*), he thus briefly characterizes.

¶ III. The Causes and Occasions of Error are comprehended in one or other of the four
following classes. For they are found
either, 1°, In the General Circum-
stances which modify the intellectual character of the individual; or, 2°, In the Constitution, Habits, and Reciprocal Relations of his powers of Cognition, Feeling, and Desire; or, 3°, In the Language which he employs, as an Instrument of Thought and a Medium of Communication: or, 4°, In the nature of the Objects themselves, about which his knowledge is conversant.

Par. III. Error,— its sources.

¶ IV. Under the General Circumstances which
modify the character of the individual
are comprehended, 1°, The particular
degree of Cultivation to which his
nation has attained; for its rudeness,
the partiality of its civilization, and
its over-refinement are all manifold occasions of error; and this cultivation is expressed not merely in the state of the arts and sciences, but in the degree of its religious, political, and social advancement; 2°, The Stricter Associations, in so far as these tend to limit the freedom of thought, and to give it a one-sided direction; such are Schools, Sects, Orders, Exclusive Societies, Corporations, Castes, etc.

Par. IV. I. General Circumstances which modify the character of the individual.

In the commencement of the Course, I had occasion to

allude to the tendency there is in man to assimilate in opinions and habits of thought to those with whom he lives. Man is by nature, not merely by accidental necessity, a social being. For only in society does he find the conditions which his different faculties require for their due development and application. But society, in all its forms and degrees, from a family to a State, is only possible under the condition of a certain harmony of sentiment among its members; and as man is by nature destined to a social existence, he is by nature determined to that analogy of thought and feeling which society supposes, and out of which society springs. There is thus in every association, great and small, a certain gravitation of opinions towards a common centre. As in our natural body every part has a necessary sympathy with every other, and all together form, by their harmonious conspiration, a healthy whole; so, in the social body, there is always a strong predisposition in each of its members to act and think in unison with the rest. This universal sympathy or fellow-feeling is the principle of the different spirit dominant in different ages, countries, ranks, sexes, and periods of life. It is the cause why fashions, why political and religious enthusiasm, why moral example either for good or evil, spread so rapidly and exert so powerful an influence. As men are naturally prone to imitate others, they, consequently, regard as important or insignificant, as honorable or disgraceful, as true or false, as good or bad, what those around them consider in the same light.

Explication. Man by nature social, and influenced by the opinions of his fellows.

Of the various testimonies I formerly quoted, of the strong assimilating influence of man on man, and of the power of custom, to make that appear true, natural, and necessary,

Pascal quoted on the power of custom.

which in reality is false, unnatural, and only accidentally suitable, I shall only adduce that of Pascal. "In the just and the unjust," says he, "we find hardly anything which does not change its character in changing its climate. Three degrees of an elevation of the pole reverses the whole of jurisprudence. A meridian is decisive of truth, and a few years, of possession. Fundamental laws change. Right has its epochs. A pleasant justice which a river or a mountain limits! Truth on this side the Pyrenees, error on the other!" It is the remark of an ingenious philosopher, "that if we take a survey of the universe, all nations will be found admiring only the reflection of their own qualities, and contemning in others whatever is contrary to what they are accustomed to meet with among themselves. Here is the Englishman accusing the French of frivolity; and here the Frenchman reproaching the Englishman with selfishness and brutality. Here is the Arab persuaded of the infallibility of his Caliph, and deriding the Tartar who believes in the immortality of the Grand Lama. In every nation we find the same congratulation of their own wisdom, and the same contempt of that of their neighbors.

"Were there a sage sent down to earth from heaven, who regulated his conduct by the dictates of pure reason alone, this sage would be universally regarded as a fool. He would be, as Socrates says, like a physician accused by the pastry-cooks, before a tribunal of children, of prohibiting the eating of tarts and cheese-cakes; a crime undoubtedly of the highest magnitude in the eyes of his judges. In vain would this sage support his opinions by the clearest arguments,—the most irrefragable demonstrations; the whole world would be for him like the nation of hunchbacks, among whom, as the Indian fabulists relate, there once upon a time appeared a god, young, beautiful, and of consummate symmetry. This god, they add, entered the capital; he was there forthwith surrounded by a crowd of natives; his figure appeared to them extraordinary; laughter, hooting, and taunts manifested their astonishment, and they were about to carry their outrages still further, had not one of the inhabitants (who had undoubtedly seen other men), in order to snatch him from the danger, suddenly cried out—' My friends! my friends! What are we going to do? Let us not insult this miserable monstrosity. If heaven has bestowed on us the general gift of beauty,—if it has adorned our backs with a mount of flesh, let us with pious gratitude repair to the temple and render our acknowledgement to the immortal gods.'" This fable is the history of human vanity. Every nation admires its own defects, and contemns the opposite qualities in its neighbors. To succeed in a country, one must be a bearer of the national hump of the people among whom he sojourns.

There are few philosophers who undertake to make their countrymen aware of the ridiculous figure they cut in the eye of reason; and still fewer the nations who are able to profit by the advice. All are so punctiliously attached to the interests of their vanity, that none obtain in any country the name of wise, except those who are fools of the common folly. There is no opinion too absurd not to find nations ready to believe it, and individuals prompt to be its executioners or its martyrs. Hence it is that the philosopher declared, that if he held all truths shut up within his hand, he would take especial care not to show

The art of doubting well difficult to teach and to learn.

them to his fellow-men. In fact, if the discovery of a single truth dragged Galileo to the prison, to what punishment would he not be doomed who should discover all? Among those who now ridicule the folly of the human intellect, and are indignant at the persecution of Galileo, there are few who would not, in the age of that philosopher, have clamored for his death. They would then have been imbued with different opinions; and opinions not more passively adopted than those which they at present vaunt as liberal and enlightened. To learn to doubt of our opinions, it is sufficient to examine the powers of the human intellect, to survey the circumstances by which it is affected, and to study the history of human follies. Yet in modern Europe six centuries elapsed from the foundation of Universities until the appearance of that extraordinary man,—I mean Descartes,—whom his age first persecuted, and then almost worshipped as a demi-god, for initiating men in the art of doubting,—of doubting well,—a lesson at which, however, both their skepticism and credulity show that, after two centuries, they are still but awkward scholars. Socrates was wont to say,—"All that I know is that I know nothing." In our age it would seem that men know everything except what Socrates knew. Our errors would not be so frequent were we less ignorant; and our ignorance more curable, did we not believe ourselves to be all-wise.

Thus it is that the influence of Society, both in its general form of a State or Nation, and in its particular forms of Schools, Sects, etc., determines a multitude of opinions in its members, which, as they are passively received, so they are often altogether erroneous.

Among the more general and influential of these there are two, which, though apparently contrary, are, however, both, in reality, founded on the same incapacity of independent thought,—on the same influence of example—I mean the excessive admiration of the Old, and the excessive admiration of the New. The former of these prejudices—under which may be reduced the prejudice in favor of Authority,—was at one time prevalent to an extent of which it is difficult for us to form a conception. This prejudice is prepared by the very education not only which we do, but which we all must receive. The child necessarily learns everything at first on credit,—he believes upon authority. But when the rule of authority is once established, the habit of passive acquiescence and belief is formed, and, once formed, it is not again always easily thrown off. When the child has grown up to an age in which he might employ his own reason, he has acquired a large stock of ideas; but who can calculate the number of errors which this stock contains? and by what means is he able to discriminate the true from the false? His mind has been formed to obedience and uninquiry; he possesses no criterion by which to judge; it is painful to suspect what has been long venerated, and it is felt even as a kind of personal mutilation to tear up what has become irradicated in his intellectual and moral being. *Ponere difficile est quæ placuere diu.* The adult does not, therefore, often judge for himself more than the child; and the tyranny of authority and foregone opinion continues to exert a sway during the whole course of his life. In our infancy and childhood the credit accorded to our parents and instructors is implicit;

Marginalia:
Two general forms of the influence of example.
1. Prejudice in favor of the Old.
Prepared by Education.

GENERAL CIRCUMSTANCES—SOCIETY. 79

and if what we have learned from them be confirmed by what we hear from others, the opinions thus recommended become at length stamped in almost indelible characters upon the mind. This is the cause why men so rarely abandon the opinions which vulgarly pass current; and why what comes as new is by so many, for its very novelty, rejected as false. And hence it is, as already noticed, that truth is as it were geographically and politically distributed; what is truth on one side of a boundary being error and absurdity on the other. What has now been said of the influence of society at large, is true also of the lesser societies which it contains, all of which impose with a stronger or feebler, a wider or more contracted, authority, certain received opinions upon the faith of the members. Hence it is that whatever has once obtained a recognition in any society, large or small, is not rejected when the reasons on which it was originally admitted have been proved erroneous. It continues, even for the reason that it is old and has been accepted, to be accepted still; and the title which was originally defective, becomes valid by continuance and prescription.

But opposed to this cause of error, from the prejudice in favor of the Old, there is the other, directly the reverse,—the prejudice in favor of the New. This prejudice may be, in part at least, the result of sympathy and fellow-feeling. This is the cause why new opinions, however erroneous, if they once obtain a certain number of converts, often spread with a rapidity and to an extent, which, after their futility has been ultimately shown, can only be explained on the principle of a kind of intellectual contagion. But the principal cause of the prejudice in favor of novelty lies in the Passions,

2. Prejudice in favor of the New.

and the consideration of these does not belong to the class of causes with which we are at present occupied.

Connected with and composed of both these prejudices,—that in favor of the old and that in favor of the new,—there is the prejudice of Learned Authority; for this is usually associated with the prejudices of Schools and Sects. As often as men have appeared, who, by the force of their genius, have opened up new views of science, and thus contributed to the progress of human intellect, so often have they, likewise, afforded the occasion of checking its advancement, and of turning it from the straight path of improvement. Not that this result is to be imputed as a reproach to them, but simply because it is of the nature of man to be so affected. The views which influenced these men of genius, and which, consequently, lie at the foundation of their works, are rarely comprehended in their totality by those who have the names of these authors most frequently in their mouths.' The many do not concern themselves to seize the ideal which a philosopher contemplated, and of which his actual works are only the imperfect representations; they appropriate to themselves only some of his detached apothegms and propositions, and of these compound, as they best can, a sort of system suited to their understanding, and which they employ as a talisman in their controversies with others. As their reason is thus a captive to authority, and, therefore, unable to exert its native freedom, they, consequently, catch up the true and the false without discrimination, and remain always at the point of progress where they had been placed by their leaders. In their hands a system of living truths becomes a

Prejudice of Learned Authority.

mere petrified organism; and they require that the whole science shall become as dead and as cold as their own idol. Such was Plato's doctrine in the hands of the Platonists; such was Aristotle's philosophy in the hands of the Schoolmen; and the history of modern systems affords equally the same result.

So much for the first genus into which the Sources of Error are divided.

LECTURE III.—MODIFIED STOICHEIOLOGY.

SECTION II.—ERROR—ITS CAUSES AND REMEDIES.

A.—GENERAL CIRCUMSTANCES—SOCIETY.

B.—AS IN POWERS OF COGNITION, FEELING, AND DESIRE.

I.—AFFECTIONS—PRECIPITANCY—SLOTH—HOPE AND FEAR—SELF-LOVE.

Recapitulation.

In our last Lecture, we entered on the consideration of the various sources of Error. These, I stated, may be conveniently reduced to four heads, and consist, 1°, In the General Circumstances which modify the intellectual character of the individual; 2°, In the Constitution, Habits, and Reciprocal Relations of his powers of Cognition, Feeling, and Desire; 3°, In the language which he employs as an Instrument of Thought and a Medium of Communication; and, 4°, In the nature of the Objects themselves about which his knowledge is conversant.

Of these, I then gave you a general view of the nature of those occasions of Error, which originate in the circumstances under the influence of which the character and opinions of man are determined for him as a member of society. Under this head I stated, that, as man is destined by his Creator to fulfil the end of his existence in society, he is wisely furnished with a disposition to imitate those among whom his lot is cast, and thus conform himself to whatever section of human society he may by birth belong, or of which he may afterwards become a member. The education we receive, nay the very possibility of receiving education at all, supposes to a certain extent the passive infusion of foreign and traditionary opinions. For as man is compelled to think much earlier than he is able to think for himself,—all education necessarily imposes on him many opinions which, whether in themselves true or false, are, in reference to the recipient, only prejudices ; and it is even only a small number of mankind who at a later period are able to bring these obtruded opinions to the test of reason, and by a free exercise of their own intelligence to reject them if found false, or to acknowledge them if proved true.

But while the mass of mankind thus remain, during their whole lives, only the creatures of the accidental circumstances which have concurred to form for them their habits and beliefs ; the few who are at last able to form opinions for themselves, are still dependent, in a great measure, on the unreasoning judgment of the many. Public opinion, hereditary custom, despotically impose on us the capricious laws of propriety and manners. The individual may possibly, in matters of science, emancipate himself from their servitude ; in the affairs of life he must quietly submit himself to the yoke. The only freedom he can here prudently manifest, is to resign himself with a consciousness that he is a slave not to reason but to conventional accident. And while he conforms himself to the usages of his own society, he will be tolerant to those of others. In this respect his maxim will be that of the Scythian prince : "With you such may be the custom—with us it is different."

So much for the general nature of the influence to which we are exposed from the circumstances of Society; it now remains to say what are the means by which this influence, as a source of error, may be counteracted.

Means by which the influence of society, as a source of error, may be counteracted.

It has been seen that, in consequence of the manner in which our opinions are formed for us by the accidents of society, our imposed and supposed knowledge is a confused medley of truths and errors. Here it is evidently necessary to institute a critical examination of the contents of this knowledge. Descartes proposes that, in order to discriminate, among our prejudiced opinions, the truths from the errors, we ought to commence by doubting all. This has exposed him to much obloquy and clamor, but most unjustly. The doctrine of Descartes has nothing skeptical or offensive; for he only maintains that it behooves us to examine all that has been inculcated on us from infancy, and under the masters to whose authority we have been subjected, with the same attention and circumspection which we accord to dubious questions. In fact there is nothing in the precept of Descartes, which had not been previously enjoined by other philosophers. Of these I formerly quoted to you several, and among others the remarkable testimonies of Aristotle, St. Augustin, and Lord Bacon.

Necessary to institute a critical examination of the contents of our knowledge.

Descartes,—his precept.

But although there be nothing reprehensible in the precept of Descartes, as enounced by him, it is of less practical utility in consequence of no account being taken of the circumstances which condition and modify its application. For, in the first place, the judgments to be

Conditions which modify its application.

examined ought not to be taken at random, but selected on a principle, and arranged in due order and dependence. But this requires no ordinary ability, and the distribution of things into their proper classes is one of the last and most difficult fruits of philosophy. In the second place, there are among our prejudices, or pretended cognitions, a great many hasty conclusions, the investigation of which requires much profound thought, skill, and acquired knowledge. Now, from both of these considerations, it is evident that to commence philosophy by such a review, it is necessary for a man to be a philosopher before he can attempt to become one. The precept of Descartes is, therefore, either unreasonable, or it is too unconditionally expressed. And this latter alternative is true.

What can be rationally required of the student of philosophy, is not a preliminary and absolute, but a gradual and progressive abrogation, of prejudices. It can only be required of him, that, when, in the course of his study of philosophy, he meets with a proposition which has not been already sufficiently sifted,—(whether it has been elaborated as a principle or admitted as a conclusion),—he should pause, discuss it without prepossession, and lay aside for future consideration all that has not been subjected to a searching scrutiny. The precept of Descartes, when rightly explained, corresponds to that of St. Paul : " If any man among you seemeth to be wise in this world, let him become a fool, that he may be wise ;" that is, let him not rely more on the opinions in which he has been brought up, and in favor of which he and those around him are prejudiced, than on so many visions of imagination ; and let him examine them with the

A gradual and progressive abrogation of prejudices all that can be required of the student of philosophy.

same circumspection as if he were assured that they contain some truth among much falsehood and many extravagances.

Proceeding now to the second class of the Sources of Error, which are found in the Mind itself, I shall commence with the following paragraph:

¶ V. The Sources of Error which arise from the Constitution, Habits, and Reciprocal Relations of the powers of Cognition, Feeling, and Desire, may be subdivided into two kinds. The first of these consists in the undue preponderance of the Affective Elements of mind (the Desires and Feelings) over the Cognitive; the second, in the weakness or inordinate strength of some one or other of the Cognitive Faculties themselves.

Par. V. II. Source of Error arising from the powers of Cognition, Feeling, and Desire,—of two kinds.

Affection is that state of mind in which the Feelings and Desires exert an influence not under the control of reason; in other words, a tendency by which the intellect is impeded in its endeavor to think an object as that object really is, and compelled to think it in conformity with some view prescribed by the passion or private interest of the subject thinking.

Explication.
I. Preponderance of Affection over Cognition.

The human mind, when unruffled by passion, may be compared to a calm sea. A calm sea is a clear mirror, in which the sun and clouds, in which the forms of heaven and earth, are reflected back precisely as they are presented. But let a wind arise, and the smooth, clear surface of the water is lifted into billows and agitated into foam. It no more reflects the sun and clouds, the forms of heaven and earth, or it reflects them only as distorted and broken images. In

Influence of Passion on the Mind.

like manner, the tranquil mind receives and reflects the world without as it truly is; but let the wind of passion blow, and every object is represented, not as it exists, but in the colors and aspects and partial phases in which it pleases the subject to regard it. The state of passion and its influence on the Cognitive Faculties are truly pictured by Boethius :—

Boethius quoted.

> " *Nubibus atris*
> *Condita nullum*
> *Fundere possunt*
> *Sidera lumen.*
> *Si mare volvens*
> *Turbidus auster*
> *Misceat œstum,*
> *Vitrea dudum,*
> *Cernere verum,*
> *Tramite recto*
> *Carpere callem :*
> *Gaudia pelle,*
> *Pelle timorem,*
>
> *Parque serenis*
> *Unda diebus,*
> *Mox resoluto*
> *Sordida cœno,*
> *Visibus obstat.*
> . . . . .
> *Tu quoque si vis*
> *Lumine claro*
> *Spemque fugato,*
> *Nec dolor adsit,*
> *Nubila mens est,*
> *Vinctaque frenis,*
> *Hœc ubi regnant.*"

Every error consists in this,—that we take something for non-existent, because we have not become aware of its existence, and that, in place of this existent something, we fill up the premises of a probable reasoning with something else.

Error limited to Probable Reasoning.

I have here limited the possibility of error to Probable Reasoning, for, in Intuition and Demonstration, there is but little Possibility of important error. Hobbes indeed asserts that had it been contrary to the interest of those in authority, that the three angles of a triangle should be equal to two right angles, this truth would have been long ago proscribed as heresy, or as high treason. This may be an ingenious illustration of the blind tendency of the passions to subjugate intelligence; but we should take it for more than was intended by its author, were we to take it as more than an ingenious exaggeration. Limiting, therefore, error to probable inference (and this constitutes, with the exception of a comparatively small department, the whole domain of human reasoning), we have to inquire, How do the Passions influence us to the assumption of false premises? To estimate the amount of probability for or against a given proposition, requires a tranquil, an unbiassed, a comprehensive consideration, in order to take all the relative elements of judgment into due account. But this requisite state of mind is disturbed when any interest, any wish, is allowed to interfere.

¶ VI. The disturbing Passions may be reduced to four: Precipitancy, Sloth, Hope and Fear, Self-love.

Par. VI. The Passions, as sources of Error,—reduced to four.

1°, A restless anxiety for a decision begets impatience, which decides before the preliminary inquiry is concluded. This is precipitancy.

2°, The same result is the effect of Sloth, which dreams on in conformity to custom, without subjecting its beliefs to the test of active observation.

3°, The restlessness of Hope or Fear impedes observation, distracts attention, or forces it only on what interests the passion;—the sanguine looking on only what harmonizes with his hopes, the diffident only on what accords with his fears.

4°, Self-love perverts our estimate of probability by causing us to rate the grounds of judgment, not according to their real influence on the truth of the decision, but according to their bearing on our personal interests therein.

In regard to Impatience or Precipitation,—"all is the cause of this which determines our choice on one side rather than another. An imagination excites pleasure, and because it excites pleasure we yield ourselves up to it. We suppose, for example, that we are all that we ought to be, and why? Because this supposition gives us pleasure. This, in some dispositions, is one of the greatest obstacles to improvement; for he who entertains it, thinks there is no necessity to labor to become what he is already. "I believe," says Seneca, "that many had it in their power to have attained to wisdom, had they not been impeded by the belief that wisdom they had already attained. '*Multos puto ad sapientiam potuisse pervenire, nisi putassent se pervenisse.*'" Erasmus gives the following as the principal advice to a young votary of learning in the conduct of his studies: " To read the most learned books, to converse with the most learned men; but, above all, never to conceit that he himself was learned."

Explication.
1. *Precipitancy.*

Seneca.

Erasmus.

"From the same cause, men flatter themselves with the hope of dying old, although few attain to longevity. The less probable the event, the more certain are they of its occurrence; and why? Because the imagination of it is agreeable. '*Decrepiti senes paucorum annorum accessionem votis mendicant; minores natu seipsos esse fingunt; mendacio sibi blandiuntur; et tam libenter fallunt, quam si fata una decipiant.*'" "Preachers," says Montaigne, "are aware that the emotion which arises during their sermons animates themselves to belief, and we are conscious that when roused to anger we apply ourselves more intently to the defence of our

Illustrations.

From Seneca.

From Montaigne.

thesis, and embrace it with greater vehemence and approbation, than we did when our mind was cool and unruffled. You simply state your case to an advocate; he replies with hesitation and doubt; you are aware that it is indifferent to him whether he undertakes the defence of the one side or of the other; but have you once fee'd him well to take your case in hand; he begins to feel an interest in it; his will is animated. His reason and his science become also animated in proportion. Your case presents itself to his understanding as a manifest and indubitable truth; he now sees it in a wholly different light, and really believes that you have law and justice on your side." It is proper to observe that Montaigne was himself a lawyer,—he had been a counsellor of the Parliament of Bordeaux.

It might seem that Precipitate Dogmatism and an inclination to Skepticism were opposite characters of mind. They are, however, closely allied, if not merely phases of the same disposition. This is indeed confessed by the Skeptic Montaigne: "The most uneasy condition for me is to be kept in suspense on urgent occasions, and to be agitated between fear and hope. Deliberation, even in things of lightest moment, is very troublesome to me; and I find my mind more put to it, to undergo the various tumbling and tossing of doubt and consultation, than to set up its rest, and to acquiesce in whatever shall happen, after the die is thrown. Few passions break my sleep; but of deliberations, the least disturbs me."

Precipitate Dogmatism and Skepticism, phases of the same disposition.

Precipitation is no incurable disease. There is for it one sure and simple remedy, if properly applied. It is only required, to speak with Confucius, manfully to restrain the wild horse of precipitancy by the curb of consideration,—

Remedy for Precipitation.

to weigh the reasons of decision, each and all, in the balance of cool investigation, not to allow ourselves to decide until a clear consciousness has declared these reasons to be true,— to be sufficient; and, finally, to throw out of account the suffrages of self-love, of prepossession, of passion, and to admit only those of reflection, of experience, and of evidence. This remedy is certain and effectual. In theory it is satisfactory, but its practical application requires a moral resolution, for the acquisition of which no precept can be given.

In the second place, "Sloth is likewise a cause of precipitation, and it deserves the more attention as it is a cause of error extremely frequent, and one of which we are ourselves less aware, and which is less notorious to others. We feel it fatiguing to continue an investigation, therefore we do not pursue it; but as it is mortifying to think that we have labored in vain, we easily admit the flattering illusion that we have succeeded. By the influence of this disposition it often happens, that, after having rejected what first presented itself,—after having rejected a second time and a third time what subsequently turned up, because not sufficiently applicable or certain, we get tired of the investigation, and perhaps put up with the fourth suggestion, which is not better, haply even worse, than the preceding; and this simply because it has come into the mind when more exhausted and less scrupulous than it was at the commencement." "The volition of that man," says Seneca, "is often frustrated, who undertakes not what is easy, but who wishes what he undertakes to be easy. As often as you attempt anything, compare together yourself, the end which you propose, and the means by which it is to be accomplished.

2. Sloth.

Seneca quoted.

For the repentance of an unfinished work will make you rash. And here it is of consequence whether a man be of a fervid or of a cold, of an aspiring or of a humble, disposition."

Its remedy. To remedy this failing it is necessary, in conformity with this advice of Seneca, to consult our forces, and the time we can afford, and the difficulty of the subjects on which we enter. We ought to labor only at intervals, to avoid the tedium and disquiet consequent on unremitted application ; and to adjourn the consideration of any thought which may please us vehemently at the moment, until the prepossession in its favor has subsided with the animation which gave it birth.

3. Hope and Fear. The two Causes of premature judgment—the affections of Impatience and Sloth—being considered, I pass on to the third principle of Passion, by which the intellect is turned aside from the path of truth,—I mean the disturbing influence of Hope and Fear. These passions, though reciprocally contrary, determine a similar effect upon the deliberations of the Understanding, and are equally unfavorable for the interest of truth. In forming a just conclusion upon a question of probable reasoning, that is, where the grounds of decision are not few, palpable, and of determinate effect,—and such questions may be said to be those alone on which differences of opinion may arise, and are, consequently, those alone which require for their solution any high degree of observation and ingenuity,—in such questions hope and fear exert a very strong and a very unfavorable influence. In these questions it is requisite, in the first place, to seek out the premises ; and, in the second, to draw the conclusion. Of these requisites the first is the more important, and it is also by far the more difficult.

Now the passions of Hope and Fear operate severally to prevent the intellect from discovering all the elements of decision, which ought to be considered in forming a correct conclusion, and cause it to take into account those only which harmonize with that conclusion to which the actuating passion is inclined. And here the passion operates in two ways. In the first place, it tends so to determine the associations of thought, that only those media of proof are suggested or called into consciousness, which support the conclusion to which the passion tends. In the second place, if the media of proof by which a counter conclusion is supported are brought before the mind, still the mind is influenced by the passion to look on their reality with doubt, and, if such cannot be questioned, to undervalue their inferential importance ; whereas it is moved to admit, without hesitation, those media of proof which favor the conclusion in the interest of our hope or fear, and to exaggerate the cogency with which they establish this result. Either passion looks exclusively to a single end, and exclusively to the means by which that single end is accomplished. Thus the sanguine temperament, or the mind under the habitual predominance of hope, sees only and magnifies all that militates in favor of the wished-for consummation, which alone it contemplates ; whereas the melancholic temperament, or the mind under the habitual predominance of fear, is wholly occupied with the dreaded issue, views only what tends to its fulfilment, while it exaggerates the possible into the probable, the probable into the certain. Thus it is that whatever conclusion we greatly hope or greatly fear, to that conclusion we are disposed to leap ; and it has become almost proverbial, that men

How Hope and Fear operate unfavorably on the Understanding.

lightly believe both what they wish, and what they dread, to be true.

But the influence of Hope on our judgments, inclining us to find whatever we wish to find, in so far as this arises from the illusion of Self-love, is comprehended in this,—the fourth cause of error,—to which I now proceed.

Self-love, under which I include the dispositions of Vanity, Pride, and, in general, all those which incline us to attribute an undue weight to those opinions in which we feel a personal interest, is by far the most extensive and influential in the way of reason and truth. In virtue of this principle, whatever is ours—whatever is adopted or patronized by us, whatever belongs to those to whom we are attached is either gratuitously clothed with a character of truth, or its pretensions to be accounted true are not scrutinized with the requisite rigor and impartiality. I am a native of this country, and, therefore, not only is its history to me a matter of peculiar interest, but the actions and character of my countrymen are viewed in a very different light from that in which they are regarded by a foreigner. I am born and bred a member of a religious sect, and because they constitute my creed, I find the tenets of this sect alone in conformity to the Word of God. I am the partisan of a philosophical doctrine, and am, therefore, disposed to reject whatever does not harmonize with my adopted system.

4. Self-love.

"It is the part of a philosopher," says Aristotle, "inasmuch as he is a philosopher, to subjugate self-love, and to refute, if contrary to truth, not only the opinions of his friends, but the doctrines which he himself may have professed." It is certain, however, that philosophers—for philosophers are

Aristotle,—his precept.

men—have been too often found to regulate their conduct by the same opposite principle. That man pretended to the name of philosopher, who scrupled not to declare that he would rather be in the wrong with Plato than in the right with his opponents. "Gisbert Voetius urged Mersennus to refute a work of Descartes' a year before the book appeared, and before he had himself the means of judging whether the opinions it contained were right or wrong. A certain professor of philosophy in Padua came to Galileo, and requested that he would explain to him the meaning of the term *parallaxis;* which he wished, he said, to refute, having heard that it was opposed to Aristotle's doctrine, touching the relative situation of the comets. 'What!' answered Galileo, 'you wish to controvert a word the meaning of which you do not know!' Redi tells us that a sturdy Peripatetic of his acquaintance would never consent to look at the heavens through a telescope, lest he should be compelled to admit the existence of the new stars discovered by Galileo and others. The same Redi informs us that he knew another Peripatetic, a staunch advocate of the Aristotlean doctrine of equivocal generation, (a doctrine, by the way, which now again divides the physiologists of Europe), and who, in particular, maintained that the green frogs which appear upon a shower come down with the rain, who would not be induced himself to select and examine one of these frogs. And why? Because he was unwilling to be convicted of his error, by Redi showing him the green matter in the stomach, and its feculæ in the intestines of the animal." The spirit of the Peripatetic philosophy was, however, wholly misunderstood by these mistaken followers of Aristotle; for a true Aristotelian is one who listens

Illustrations of the Influence of Self-love on our opinions.

rather to the voice of nature than to the precept of any master, and it is well expressed in the motto of the great French anatomist—*Riolanus est Peripateticus ; credit ea, et ea tantum, quæ vidit.* Erom the same principle proceeds the abuse, and sometimes even the persecution, which the discoverers of new truths encounter from those who cherished opinions these truths subvert.

In like manner, as we are disposed to maintain our own opinion, we are inclined to regard with favor the opinions of those to whom we are attached by love, gratitude, and other conciliatory affections. "We do not limit our attachment to the persons of our friends,—we love in a certain sort all that belongs to them ; and as men generally manifest sufficient ardor in support of their opinions, we are led insensibly by a kind of sympathy to credit, to approve, and to defend these also, and that even more passionately than our friends themselves. We bear affection to others for various reasons. The agreement of tempers, of inclinations, of pursuits ; their appearance, their manners, their virtue, the partiality which they have shown to us, the services we have received at their hands, and many other particular causes, determine and direct our love.

<small>Self-love leads us to regard with favor the opinions of those to whom we are in any way attached.</small>

" It is observed by the great Malebranche, that if any of our friends,—any even of those we are disposed to love,—advance an opinion, we forthwith lightly allow ourselves to be persuaded of its truth. This opinion we accept and support, without troubling ourselves to inquire whether it be conformable to fact, frequently even against our conscience, in conformity to the darkness and confusion of our intellect, to

<small>Malebranche adduced to this effect.</small>

the corruption of our heart, and to the advantages which we hope to reap from our facility and complaisance."

The influence of this principle is seen still more manifestly when the passion changes; for though the things themselves remain unaltered, our judgments concerning them are totally reversed. How often do we behold persons who cannot, or will not, recognize a single good quality in an individual from the moment he has chanced to incur their dislike, and who are even ready to adopt opinions, merely because opposed to others maintained by the object of their aversion? The celebrated Arnauld goes so far even as to assert, that men are naturally envious and jealous; that it is with pain they endure the contemplation of others in the enjoyment of advantages which they do not themselves possess; and, as the knowledge of truth and the power of enlightening mankind is one of these, that they have a secret inclination to deprive them of that glory. This accordingly often determines them to controvert without a ground the opinions and discoveries of others. Self-love accordingly often argues thus:—'This is an opinion which I have originated, this is an opinion, therefore, which is true;' whereas the natural malignity of man not less frequently suggests such another: 'It is another than I who has advanced this doctrine; this doctrine is, therefore, false.'

This shown especially when the passion changes.

Arnauld holds that man is naturally envious.

We may distinguish, however, from malignant or envious contradiction another passion, which, though more generous in its nature and not simply a mode of Self-love, tends, nevertheless, equally to divert us from the straight road of truth,—I mean Pugnacity, or the love of Disputation.

The love of Disputation.

Under the influence of this passion, we propose as our end victory, not truth. We insensibly become accustomed to find a reason for any opinion, and, in placing ourselves above all reasons, to surrender our belief to none. Thus it is why two disputants so rarely ever agree, and why a question is seldom or never decided in a discussion, where the combative dispositions of the reasoners have once been roused in activity. In controversy it is always easy to find wherewithal to reply; the end of the parties is not to avoid error, but to impose silence; and they are less ashamed of continuing wrong than of confessing that they are not right.

<small>These affections the immediate causes of all error.

Preliminary conditions requisite for the efficiency of precepts against the sources of error.</small>

These affections may be said to be the immediate causes of all error. Other causes there are, but not immediate. In so far as Logic detects the sources of our false judgments and shows their remedies, it must carefully inculcate that no precautionary precept for particular cases can avail, unless the inmost principle of the evil be discovered, and a cure applied. You must, therefore, as you would remain free from the hallucination of false opinion, be convinced of the absolute necessity of following out the investigation of every question calmly and without passion. You must learn to pursue, and to estimate, truth without distraction or bias. To this there is required, as a primary condition, the unshackled freedom of thought, the equal glance which can take in the whole sphere of observation, the cool determination to pursue the truth whithersoever it may lead; and, what is still more important, the disposition to feel an interest in truth and in truth alone. If perchance some collateral interest may first prompt us to the inquiry, in our general interest for truth we must repress,—we must forget, this interest, until the inquiry be concluded. Of what account are the most venerated opinions if they be untrue? At best they are only venerable delusions. He who allows himself to be actuated in his scientific procedure by any partial interest, can never obtain a comprehensive survey of the whole he has to take into account, and always, therefore, remains incapable of discriminating, with accuracy, error from truth. The independent thinker must, in all his inquiries, subject himself to the genius of truth,—must be prepared to follow her footsteps without faltering or hesitation. In the consciousness that truth is the noblest of ends, and that he pursues this end with honesty and devotion, he will dread no consequences,—for he relies upon the truth. Does he compass the truth, he congratulates himself upon his success; does he fall short of its attainment, he knows that even his present failure will ultimately advance him to the reward he merits. Err he may, and that perhaps frequently, but he will never deceive himself. We cannot, indeed, rise superior to our limitary nature, we cannot, therefore, be reproached for failure; but we are always responsible for the calmness and impartiality of our researches, and these alone render us worthy of success. But though it be manifest, that to attain the truth we must follow whithersoever the truth may lead, still men in general are found to yield not an absolute, but only a restricted, obedience to the precept. They capitulate, and do not unconditionally surrender. I give up, but my cherished dogma in religion must not be canvassed, says one;—my political principles are above inquiry, and must be exempted, says a second;—my country is the land of lands, this cannot be disallowed, cries a third;—my order, my vocation, is undoubtedly the noblest, exclaim a fourth and fifth;—only do not require that we should confess our having erred, is the condition which many insist on stipulating. Above all, that resolve of mind is difficult, which is ready to surrender all fond convictions, and is prepared to recommence investigation the moment that a fundamental error in the former system of belief has been detected. These are the principal grounds why, among men, opinion is so widely separated from opinion; and why the clearest demonstration is so frequently for a season frustrated of victory.

<small>Par. VII. Rules against Errors from the Affections.</small> ¶ VII. Against the Errors which arise from the Affections, there may be given the three following rules:

1°, When the error has arisen from the influence of an active affection, the decisive judgment is to be annulled; the mind is then to be freed, as far as possible, from passion, and the process of inquiry to be recommenced as soon as the requisite tranquility has been restored.

2°, When the error has arisen from a relaxed enthusiasm for knowledge, we must reanimate this interest by a vivid representation of the paramount dignity of truth, and of the lofty destination of our intellectual nature.

3°, In testing the accuracy of our judgments, we must be particularly suspicious of those results which accord with our private inclinations and predominant tendencies.

These rules require no comment.

LECTURE IV.—MODIFIED STOICHEIOLOGY.

SECTION II.—ERROR,—ITS CAUSES AND REMEDIES.

B.—AS IN THE COGNITIONS, FEELINGS, AND DESIRES.

II.—WEAKNESS AND DISPROPORTIONED STRENGTH OF THE FACULTIES OF KNOWLEDGE.

I NOW go on to the Second Head of the class of Errors founded on the Natural Constitution, the Acquired Habits, and the Reciprocal Relations of our Cognitive and Affective Powers, that is, to the Causes of Error which originate in the Weakness or Disproportioned Strength of one or more of our Faculties of Knowledge themselves.

Weakness and Disproportioned Strength of the Faculties of Knowledge.

Here, in the first place, I might consider the errors which have arisen from the Limited Nature of the Human Intellect in general,— or rather from the mistakes that have been made by philosophers in denying or not taking this limited nature into account. The illustration of this subject is one which is relative to, and supposes an acquaintance with, some of the abstrucest speculations in Philosophy, and which belong not to Logic, but to Metaphysics. I shall not, therefore, do more than

Neglect of the Limited Nature of the Human Intellect a source of error.

simply indicate at present, what it will be proper at another season fully to explain. It is manifest, that, if the human mind be limited,—if it only knows as it is conscious, and if it be only conscious, as it is conscious of contrast and opposition, of an ego and non-ego,—if this supposition, I say, be correct, it is evident that those philosophers are in error, who virtually assume that the human mind is unlimited, that is, that the human mind is capable of a knowledge superior to consciousness,—a cognition in which knowledge and existence—the Ego and non-Ego—God and the creature—are identical; that is, of an act in which the mind is the Absolute, and knows the Absolute. This philosophy, the statement of which, as here given, it would require a long commentary to make you understand, is one which has for many years been that dominant in Germany; it is called the *Philosophy of the Absolute*, or the *Philosophy of Absolute Identity*. This system, of which Schelling and Hegel are the great representatives, errs by denying the limitation of human intelligence without proof, and by boldly building its edifice on this gratuitous negation.

<small>1. Philosophy of the Absolute.</small>

But there are other forms of philosophy which err not in actually postulating the infinity of mind, but in taking only a one-sided view of its finitude. It is a general fact, which seems, however, to have escaped the observation of philosophers, that whatever we can positively compass in thought,—whatever we can conceive as possible,—in a word, the *omne cogitabile*, lies between two extremes or poles, contradictorily opposed, and one of which must consequently be true, but of neither of which repugnant opposites are we able to represent to our mind the possibility. To take one

<small>2. A one-sided view of the finitude of mind.</small>

example out of many: we cannot construe to the mind as possible the absolute commencement of time; but we are equally unable to think the possibility of the counter alternative,—its infinite or absolute non-commencement, in other words, the infinite regress of time. Now it is evident, that, if we looked merely at the one of these contradictory opposites and argued thus: whatever is inconceivable is impossible, the absolute commencement of time is inconceivable, therefore the absolute commencement of time is impossible; but on the principles of Contradiction and Excluded Middle, one or other of the two opposite contradictories must be true; therefore, as the absolute commencement of time is impossible, the absolute or infinite non-commencement of time is necessary:—I say, it is evident that this reasoning would be incompetent and onesided, because it might be converted; for, by the same onesided process, the opposite conclusion might be drawn in favor of the absolute commencement of time.

Illustrated by reference to the two contradictories,—the absolute commencement, and the infinite non-commencement of Time.

Now, the unilateral and incompetent reasoning which I have here supposed in the case of time, is one of which the Necessitarian is guilty in his argument to prove the impossibility of human volitions being free. He correctly lays down, as the foundation of his reasoning, two propositions which must at once be allowed: 1°, That the notion of the liberty of volition involves the supposition of an absolute commencement of volition, that is, of a volition which is a cause, but is not itself, *qua* cause, an effect. 2°, That the absolute commencement of a volition, or of aught else, cannot be conceived,

The same principle exemplified in the case of the Necessitarian Argument against the Freedom of the Human Will.

that is, cannot be directly or positively thought as possible. So far he is correct; but when he goes on to apply these principles by arguing (and be it observed this syllogism lies at the root of all the reasonings for necessity), *Whatsoever is inconceivable is impossible; but the supposition of the absolute commencement of volition is inconceivable; therefore, the supposition of the absolute commencement of volition (the condition of free-will) is impossible,*—we may here demur to the sumption, and ask him,—Can he positively conceive the opposite contradictory of the absolute commencement, that is, an infinite series of relative non-commencements? If he answers, as he must, that he cannot, we may again ask him,—By what right he assumed as a self-evident axiom for his sumption, the proposition—that *whatever is inconceivable is impossible,* or by what right he could subsume his minor premise, when by his own confession he allows that the opposite contradictory of his minor premise, that is, the very proposition he is apagogically proving, is, likewise, inconceivable, and, therefore, on the principle of his sumption, likewise impossible.

The same inconsequence would equally apply to the Libertarian, who should attempt to prove that free-will must be allowed, on the ground that its contradictory opposite is impossible, because inconceivable. He cannot prove his thesis by such a process; in fact, by all speculative reasoning from the conditions of thought, the two doctrines are *in æquilibrio;*—both are equally possible,—both are equally inconceivable. It is only when the Libertarian descends to arguments drawn from the fact of the Moral Law and its conditions, that he

And in the case of the Libertarian Argument in behalf of Free-will.

is able to throw in reasons which incline the balance in his favor.

On these matters I, however, at present, only touch, in order to show you under what head of Error these reasonings would naturally fall.

<small>Weakness or disproportioned strength of the several Cognitive Faculties,—a source of Error.</small>

Leaving, therefore, or adjourning, the consideration of the imbecility of the human intellect in general, I shall now take into view, as a source of logical error, the Weakness or Disproportioned Strength of the several Cognitive Faculties. Now, as the Cognitive Faculties in man consist partly of certain Lower Powers, which he possesses in common with other sensible existences, namely, the Presentative, the Retentive, the Representative and the Reproductive Faculties, and partly of certain higher Powers, in virtue of which he enters into the rank of intelligent existences, namely, the Elaborative and Regulative Faculties,—it will be proper to consider the powers of these two classes severally in succession, in so far as they may afford the causes or occasions of error.

<small>Cognitive Faculties of two classes, a Lower and a Higher.</small>

Of the lower class, the first faculty in order is the Presentative or Acquisitive Faculty. This, as you remember, is divided into two, viz., into the Faculty which presents us with the phenomena of the outer world, and into the faculty which presents us with the phenomena of the inner. The former is External Perception, or External Sense; the latter is Self-consciousness, Internal Perception, or Internal Sense. I commence, therefore, with the Faculty of External Perception, in relation to which I give you the following paragraph :

<small>I. The Lower Class, —1. The Presentative Faculty.</small>

6*

¶ VII. When aught is presented through the outer senses, there are two conditions necessary for its adequate perception:— 1°, The relative Organs must be present, and in a condition to discharge their functions; and 2°, The objects themselves must bear a certain relation to these organs, so that the latter shall be suitably affected, and thereby the former suitably apprehended. It is possible, therefore, that, partly through the altered condition of the organs, partly through the altered situation of the objects, dissimilar presentations of the same, and similar presentations of different, objects, may be the result.

<small>Par. VII. (a) External Perception,— as a source of Error.</small>

In the first place, without the organs specially subservient to External Perception,—without the eye, the ear, etc., sensible perceptions of a precise and determinate character, such, for example, as color or sound, are not competent to man. In the second place, to perform their functions, these organs must be in a healthy or normal state; for if this condition be not fulfilled, the presentations which they furnish are null, incomplete, or false. But, in the third place, even if the organs of sense are sound and perfect, the objects to be presented and perceived must stand to these organs in a certain relation,—must bear to them a certain proportion; for, otherwise, the objects cannot be presented at all, or cannot be perceived without illusion. The sounds, for example, which we are to hear, must neither be too high nor too low in quality; the bodies which we are to see, must neither be too near nor too distant,—must neither be too feebly nor too intensely illuminated. In relation to the second condition,

<small>Explication. Conditions of the adequate activity of External Perception.</small>

there are given, in consequence of the altered state of the organs, on the one hand, different present-
Possible illusions of the Senses. ations of the same object;—thus to a person who has waxed purblind, his friend appears as an utter stranger, the eye now presenting its objects with less clearness and distinctness. On the other hand, there are given the same, or undistinguishably similar, presentations of different objects;—thus to a person in the jaundice, all things are presented yellow. In relation to the third condition, from the altered position of objects, there are, in like manner, determined, on the one hand, different presentations of the same objects,— as when the stick which appears straight in the air appears crooked when partially immersed in water; and, on the other hand, identical presentations of different objects, as when a man and a horse appear in the distance to be so similar, that the one cannot be discriminated from the other. In all these cases, these illusions are determined,—illusions which may easily become the occasions of false judgments.

In regard to the detection of such illusions and obviating the error to which they lead, it be-
Precautions with a view to the detection of illusions of the Senses, and obviating the errors to which they lead. hooves us to take the following precautions. We must, in the first place, examine the state of the organ. If found defective, we must endeavor to restore it to perfection; but if this cannot be done, we must ascertain the extent and nature of the evil, in order to be upon our guard in regard to quality and degree of the false presentation.

In the second place, we must examine the relative situation of the object, and if this be not accommodated to the organ, we must either obviate the disproportion and remove the media which occasion the illusion, or repeat the observation under different circumstances, compare these, and thus obtain the means of making an ideal abstraction of the disturbing causes.

In regard to the other Presentative Faculty,—the Faculty of Self-consciousness,—Internal Perception, or Internal Sense, as we know less of the material conditions which modify its action, we are unable to ascertain so precisely the nature of the illusions of which it may be the source. In reference to this subject you may take the following paragraph:

¶ VIII. The faculty of Self-consciousness, or Internal Sense, is subject to various changes, which either modify our apprehensions of objects, or influence the manner in which we judge concerning them. In so far, therefore, as false judgments are thus occasioned, Self-consciousness is a source of error.

Par. VIII. (b) Self-consciousness,—as a source of Error.

It is a matter of ordinary observation, that the vivacity with which we are conscious of the various phenomena of mind, differs not only at different times, in different states of health, and in different degrees of mental freshness and exhaustion, but, at the same time, differs in regard to the different kinds of these phenomena themselves. According to the greater or less intensity of this faculty, the same thoughts of which we are conscious are, at one time, clear and distinct, at another, obscure and confused. At one time we are almost wholly incapable of reflection, and every act of self attention is forced and irksome, and differences the most marked pass unnoticed; while, at another our self-consciousness is alert, all its applications pleasing,

Explication. Self-consciousness varies in intensity.

WEAKNESS OF FACULTIES OF KNOWLEDGE. 109

and the most faint and fugitive phenomena arrested and observed. On one occasion, Self-consciousness, as a reflective cognition, is strong; on another, all reflection is extinguished in the intensity of the direct consciousness of feeling or desire. In one state of mind our representations are feeble; in another, they are so lively that they are mistaken for external realities. Our self-consciousness may thus be the occasion of frequent error; for, according to its various modifications, we may form the most opposite judgments concerning the same things,—pronouncing them, for example, now to be agreeable, now to be disagreeable, according as our Internal Sense is variously affected.

The next is the Retentive or Conservative Faculty,—Memory strictly so called; in reference to which I give you the following paragraph:

¶ IX. Memory, or the Conservative Faculty, is the occasion of Error, both when too weak and when too strong. When too weak, the complement of cognitions which it retains is small and indistinct, and the Understanding or Elaborative Faculty is, consequently, unable adequately to judge concerning the similarity and differences of its representations and concepts. When too strong, the Understanding is overwhelmed with the multitude of acquired cognitions simultaneously forced upon it, so that it is unable calmly and deliberately to compare and discriminate these.

Par. IX. 2. Memory,—as a source of Error.

That both these extremes,—that both the insufficient and the superfluous vigor of the Conservative Faculty are severally the sources of Error, it will not require many observations to make apparent.

Explication.

In regard to a feeble memory, it is manifest that a multitude of false judgments must inevitably arise from an incapacity in this faculty to preserve the observations committed to its keeping. In consequence of this incapacity, if a cognition be not wholly lost, it is lost at least in part, and the circumstances of time, place, persons and things confounded with each other. For example,—I may recollect the tenor of a passage I have read, but from defect of memory may attribute to one author what really belongs to another. Thus a botanist may judge two different plants to be identical in species, having forgotten the differential characters by which they were discriminated ; or he may hold the same plant to be two different species, having examined it at different times and places.

Feeble Memory.

Though nothing could be more erroneous than a general and unqualified decision, that a great memory is incompatible with a sound judgment, yet it is an observation confirmed by the experience of all ages and countries, not only that a great memory is no condition of high intellectual talent, but that great memories are very frequently found in combination with comparatively feeble powers of thought. The truth seems to be, that where a vigorous memory is conjoined with a vigorous intellect, not only does the force of the subsidiary faculty not detract from the strength of the principal, but, on the contrary, tends to confer on it a still higher power]; whereas when the inferior faculty is disproportionately strong, that so far from nourishing and corroborating the superior, it tends to reduce this faculty to a lower level than that at which it would have stood, if united with a less overpowering subsidiary. The greater the magazine of

Strong Memory.

various knowledge which the memory contains, the better for the understanding, provided the understanding can reduce this various knowledge to order and subjection. A great memory is the principal condition of bringing before the mind many different representations and notions at once, or in rapid succession. This simultaneous or nearly simultaneous presence disturbs, however, the tranquil comparison of a small number of ideas, which, if it shall judge aright, the intellect must contemplate with a fixed and steady attention. Now, where an intellect possesses the power of concentration in a high degree, it will not be harrassed in its meditations by the officious intrusions of the subordinate faculties, however vigorous these in themselves may be, but will control their vigor by exhausting in its own operations the whole applicable energy of mind. Whereas where the inferior is more vigorous than the superior, it will, in like manner, engross in its own function the disposable amount of activity, and overwhelm the principal faculty with materials, many even in proportion as it is able to elaborate few. This appears to me the reason why men of strong memories are so often men of proportionally weak judgments, and why so many errors arise from the possession of a faculty, the perfection of which ought to exempt them from many mistaken judgments.

As to the remedy for these opposite extremes. The former— the imbecility of memory—can only be alleviated by invigorating the capacity of Retention through mnemonic exercises and methods; the latter,—the inordinate vigor of Memory,—by cultivating the Understanding to the neglect of the Conservative Faculty. It will, likewise, be necessary to be upon our guard against the errors originating in these

<small>Remedies for these opposite extremes.</small>

counter sources. In the one case distrusting the accuracy of facts, in the other, the accuracy of their elaboration.

The next faculty is the Reproductive. This, when its operation is voluntarily exerted, is called *Recollection* or *Reminiscence;* when it energizes spontaneously or without volition, it is called *Suggestion.* The laws by which it is governed in either case, but especially in the latter, are called the *Laws of Mental Association.* This Reproductive Faculty, like the Retentive, is the cause of error, both if its vigor be defective, or if it be too strong. I shall consider Recollection and Suggestion severally and apart. In regard to the former I give you the following paragraph.

3. The Reproductive Faculty.

¶ X. The Reproductive Faculty, in so far as it is voluntarily exercised, as Reminiscence, becomes a source of Error, as it is either too sluggish or too prompt, precisely as the Retentive Faculty, combined with which it constitutes Memory in the looser signification.

Par. X. (a) Reminiscence—as a source of Error.

It is necessary to say very little in special reference to Reminiscence, for what was said in regard to the Conservative Faculty or Memory Proper in its highest vigor, was applicable to, and in fact supposed a corresponding degree of, the Reproductive. For, however great may be the mass of cognitions retained in the mind, that is, out of consciousness, but potentially capable of being called into consciousness, these can never of themselves oppress the Understanding by their simultaneous crowding or rapid succession, if the faculty by which they are revoked into consciousness be inert; whereas if this revocative faculty

Explication. Reminiscence,—its undue activity.

be comparatively alert and vigorous, a smaller magazine of retained cognitions may suffice to harass the intellect with a ceaseless supply of materials too profuse for its capacity of elaboration.

On the other hand, the inactivity of our Recollection is a source of error, precisely as the weakness of our Memory proper; for it is of the same effect in relation to our judgments, whether the cognitions requisite for a decision be not retained in the mind, or whether, being retained, they are not recalled into consciousness by Reminiscence.

Its inactivity.

In regard to Suggestion, or the Reproductive Faculty operating spontaneously, that is, not in subservience to an act of Will,—I shall give you the following paragraph :

¶ XI. As our Cognitions, Feelings, and Desires are connected together by what are called the *Laws of Association*, and as each link in the chain of thought suggests or awakens into consciousness some other in conformity to these Laws,—these Laws, as they bestow a strong subjective connection on thoughts and objects of a wholly arbitrary union, frequently occasion great confusion and error in our judgments.

Par. XI. (b) Suggestion—as a source of Error.

Even in methodical thinking, we do not connect all our thoughts intentionally and rationally, but many press forward into the train, either in consequence of some external impression, or in virtue of certain internal relations, which, however, are not of a logical dependency. Thus thoughts tend to suggest each other, which have reference to things of which we were previously cognizant as coëxistent, or as immediately con-

Explication.

sequent, which have been apprehended as bearing a resemblance to each other, or which have stood together in reciprocal and striking contrast. This connection, though precarious and non-logical, is thus, however, governed by certain laws, which have been called the *Laws of Association*. These laws, which I have just enumerated, viz., the Law of Coëxistence or Simultaneity, the Law of Continuity or Immediate Succession, the Law of Similarity, and the Law of Contrast, are all only special modifications of one general law, which I would call the *Law of Redintegration;* that is, the principle according to which whatever has previously formed a part of one total act of consciousness, tends, when itself recalled into consciousness, to reproduce along with it the other parts of that original whole. But though these tendencies be denominated *laws*, the influence which they exert, though often strong and sometimes irresistible, is only contingent; for it frequently happens that thoughts which have previously stood to each other in one or other of the four relations do not suggest each other. The Laws of Association stand, therefore, on a very different footing from the laws of logical connection. But those Laws of Association, contingent though they be, exert a great and often a very pernicious influence upon thought, inasmuch as by the involuntary intrusion of representations into the mental chain which are wholly irrelevant to the matter in hand, there arises a perplexed and redundant tissue of thought, into which false characters may easily find admission, and in which true characters may easily be overlooked. But this is not all. For, by being once blended together in our consciousness, things really distinct in their nature tend again naturally to reassociate, and, at every repetition of this conjunction, this tendency is fortified, and their mutual suggestion rendered more certain and irresistible.

It is in virtue of this principle of Association and Custom, that things are clothed by us with the precarious attributes of deformity or beauty; and some philosophers have gone so far as to maintain that our principles of Taste are exclusively dependent on the accidents of Association. But if this be an exaggeration, it is impossible to deny that Association enjoys an extensive jurisdiction in the empire of taste, and, in particular, that fashion is almost wholly subject to its control.

Influence of Association in matters of Taste.

On this subject I may quote a few sentences from the first volume of Mr. Stewart's *Elements*. " In matters of Taste, the effects which we consider are produced on the mind itself, and are accompanied either with pleasure or with pain. Hence the tendency to casual association is much stronger than it commonly is with respect to physical events; and when such associations are once formed, as they do not lead to any important inconvenience, similar to those which result from physical mistakes, they are not so likely to be corrected by mere experience, unassisted by study. To this it is owing that the influence of association on our judgments concerning beauty and deformity, is still more remarkable than on our speculative conclusions; a circumstance which has led some philosophers to suppose that association is sufficient to account for the origin of these notions, and that there is no such thing as a standard of taste, founded on the principles of the human constitution. But this is undoubtedly pushing the theory a great deal too far. The association of ideas can never account for the origin of a

Stewart quoted.

new notion, or of a pleasure essentially different from all the others which we know. It may, indeed, enable us to conceive how a thing indifferent in itself may become a source of pleasure, by being connected in the mind with something else which is naturally agreeable; but it presupposes, in every instance, the existence of those notions and those feelings which it is its province to combine; insomuch that, I apprehend, it will be found, wherever associations produce a change in our judgments on matters of taste, it does so by co-operating with some natural principle of the mind, and implies the existence of certain original sources of pleasure and uneasiness.

"A mode of dress, which at first appeared awkward, acquires, in a few weeks or months, the appearance of elegance. By being accustomed to see it worn by those whom we consider as models of taste, it becomes associated with the agreeable impressions which we receive from the ease and grace and refinement of their manners. When it pleases by itself, the effect is to be ascribed, not to the object actually before us, but to the impressions with which it has been generally connected, and which it naturally recalls to the mind.

"This observation points out the cause of the perpetual vicissitudes in dress, and in everything whose chief recommendation arises from fashion. It is evident that, as far as the agreeable effect of an ornament arises from association, the effect will continue only while it is confined to the higher orders. When it is adopted by the multitude, it not only ceases to be associated with ideas of taste and refinement, but it is associated with ideas of affectation, absurd imitation, and vulgarity. It is accordingly laid aside by the higher orders, who studiously avoid every circumstance in external appearance which is debased by low and common use; and they are led to exercise their invention in the introduction of some new peculiarities, which first become fashionable, then common, and last of all, are abandoned as vulgar.

"Our moral judgments, too, may be modified, and even perverted to a certain degree, in consequence of the operation of the same principle. In the same manner in which a person who is regarded as a model of taste may introduce, by his example, an absurd or fantastical dress; so a man of splendid virtues may attract some esteem also to his imperfections; and, if placed in a conspicuous situation, may render his vices and follies objects of general imitation among the multitude.

"'In the reign of Charles II.,' says Mr. Smith, 'a degree of licentiousness was deemed the characteristic of a liberal education. It was connected, according to the notions of those times, with generosity, sincerity, magnanimity, loyalty; and proved that the person who acted in this manner was a gentleman, and not a puritan. Severity of manners, and regularity of conduct, on the other hand, were altogether unfashionable, and were connected, in the imagination of that age, with cant, cunning, hypocrisy, and low manners. To superficial minds the vices of the great seem at all times agreeable. They connect them not only with the splendor of fortune, but with many superior virtues which they ascribe to their superiors; with the spirit of freedom and independency; with frankness, generosity, humanity, and politeness. The virtues of the inferior ranks of people, on the contrary,—their parsimonious frugality, their painful industry, and rigid adherence to rules, seem to them mean and disagreeable. They connect them both with the meanness of the station to which these qualities commonly belong, and with many great vices which they suppose usually accompany them; such as an abject, cowardly, ill-natured, lying, pilfering disposition.'"

"In general," says Condillac, "the impression we experience in the different circumstances of life, makes us associate ideas with a force which renders them ever after for us indissoluble.

<small>Condillac quoted on the influence of Association.</small>

We cannot, for example, frequent the society of our fellow-men without insensibly associating the notions of certain intellectual or moral qualities with certain corporeal characters. This is the reason why persons of a decided physiognomy please or displease us more than others; for a physiognomy is only an assemblage of characters, with which we have associated notions which are not suggested without an accompaniment of satisfaction or disgust. It is not, therefore, to be marvelled at that we judge men according to their physiognomy, and that we sometimes feel towards them at first sight aversion or inclination. In consequence of these associations, we are often vehemently prepossessed in favor of certain individuals, and no less violently disposed against others. It is because all that strikes us in our friends or in our enemies is associated with the agreeable or the disagreeable feeling which we severally experience; and because the faults of the former borrow always something pleasing from their amiable qualities; whereas the amiable qualities of the latter seem always to participate of their vices. Hence it is that these associations exert a powerful influence on our whole conduct. They foster our love or hatred; enhance our esteem or contempt; excite our gratitude or indignation; and produce those sympathies,—those antipathies, or those capricious inclinations, for which we are sometimes sorely puzzled to render a reason. Descartes tells us that through life he had always found a strong predilection for squint eyes,—which he explains by the circumstance, that the nursery-maid by whom he had been kindly tended, and to whom as a child he was, consequently, much attached, had this defect." 'S Gravesande, I think it is, who tells us he knew a man, and a man otherwise of sense, who had a severe fall from a waggon; and thereafter he could never enter a waggon without fear and trembling, though he daily used, without apprehension, another and far more dangerous vehicle. A girl once and again sees her mother or maid fainting and vociferating at the appearance of a mouse; if she has afterwards to escape from danger, she will rather pass through flames than take a patent way, if obstructed by a *ridiculus mus*. A remarkable example of the false judgments arising from this principle of association, is recorded by Herodotus and Justin, in reference to the war of the Scythians with their slaves. The slaves, after they had repeatedly repulsed several attacks with arms, were incontinently put to flight when their masters came out against them with their whips.

I shall now offer an observation in regard to the appropriate remedy for this evil influence of Association

The only mean by which we can become aware of, counteract, and overcome, this besetting weakness of our nature, is Philosophy,— the Philosophy of the Human Mind; and this studied both in the consciousness of the individual, and in the history of the species. The philosophy of mind, as studied in the consciousness of the individual, exhibits to us the source and

[margin: Only remedy for the influence of Association is the Philosophy of the Human Mind.]

nature of the illusion. It accustoms us to discriminate the casual, from the necessary, combinations of thought; it sharpens and corroborates our faculties, encourages our reason to revolt against the blind preformations of opinion, and finally enables us to break through the enchanted circle within which Custom and Association had enclosed us. But in the accomplishment of this end, we are greatly aided by the study of man under the various circumstances which have concurred in modifying his intellectual and moral character. In the great spectacle of history, we behold in different ages and countries the predominance of different systems of association, and these ages and countries are, consequently, distinguished by the prevalence of different systems of opinions. But all is not fluctuating; and, amid the ceaseless changes of accidental circumstances and precarious beliefs, we behold some principles ever active, and some truths always commanding a recognition. We thus obtain the means of discriminating, in so far as our unassisted reason is conversant about mere worldly concerns, between what is of universal and necessary certainty, and what is only of local and temporary acceptation; and, in reference to the latter, in witnessing the influence of an arbitrary association in imposing the most irrational opinions on our fellow-men, our eyes are opened, and we are warned of the danger from the same illusion to ourselves. And as the philosophy of man affords us at once the indication and the remedy of this illusion, so the philosophy of man does this exclusively and alone. Our irrational associations, our habits of groundless credulity and of arbitrary scepticism, find no medicine in the study of aught beyond the domain of mind itself.

As Goethe has well observed, "Mathematics remove no

prejudice; they cannot mitigate obstinacy, or temper party-spirit;" in a word, as to any moral influence upon the mind, they are absolutely null. Hence we may well explain the aversion of Socrates for these studies, if carried beyond a very limited extent.

The next faculty in order is the Representative, or Imagination Proper, which consists in the greater or less power of holding up an ideal object in the light of consciousness.

<small>The Representative Faculty, or Imagination Proper.</small>

The energy of Representation, though dependent on Retention and Reproduction, is not to be identified with these operations. For though these three functions (I mean Retention, Reproduction, and Representation) immediately suppose, and are immediately dependent on each other, they are still manifestly discriminated as different qualities of mind, inasmuch as they stand to each other in no determinate proportion. We find, for example, in some individuals the capacity of Retention strong, but the Reproductive and Representative Faculties sluggish and weak. In others, again, the Conservative tenacity is feeble, but the Reproductive and Representative energies prompt and vivid; while in others the power of Reproduction may be vigorous, but what is recalled is never pictured in a clear and distinct consciousness. It will be generally, indeed, admitted, that a strong retentive memory does not infer a prompt recollection; and still more that a strong memory and a prompt recollection do not infer a vivid imagination. These, therefore, though variously confounded by philosophers, we are warranted, I think, in viewing as elementary qualities of mind, which ought to be theoretically distinguished. Limiting, therefore, the term *Imagination* to the mere Faculty of Representing in a more or less vivacious manner an ideal object,—this Faculty is the source of errors which I shall comprise in the following paragraph.

¶ XII. Imagination, or the Faculty of Representing with more or less vivacity a recalled object of cognition, is the source of Errors, both when it is too languid and when it is too vigorous. In the former case, the object is respresented obscurely and indistinctly; in the latter, the ideal representation affords the illusive appearance of a sensible presentation.

Par. XII. 4. Imagination,—as a source of Error.

A strong imagination, that is, the power of holding up any ideal object to the mind in clear and steady colors, is a faculty necessary to the poet and to the artist; but not to them alone. It is almost equally requisite for the successful cultivation of every scientific pursuit; and, though differently applied, and different in the character of its representation, it may well be doubted whether Aristotle did not possess as powerful an imagination as Homer. The vigor and perfection of this faculty is seen, not so much in the representation of individual objects and fragmentary sciences, as in the representation of systems. In the better ages of antiquity the perfection, the beauty, of all works of taste, whether in Poetry, Eloquence, Sculpture, Painting, or Music, was principally estimated from the symmetry or proportion of all the parts to each other, and to the whole which they together constituted; and it was only in subservience to this general harmony that the beauty of the several parts was appreciated. In the criticism of modern times, on the contrary, the reverse is true; and we are disposed to look more to the obtrusive

Explication. Necessity of Imagination in scientific pursuits.

Diverse characteristics of art in ancient and modern times.

qualities of details, than to the keeping and unison of a whole. Our works of art are, in general, like kinds of assorted patch-work;—not systems of parts all subdued in conformity to one ideal totality, but coördinations of independent fragments, among which a *"purpureus pannus"* seldom comes amiss. The reason of this difference in taste seems to be, what at first sight may seem the reverse, that in antiquity not the Reason but the Imagination was the more vigorous;—that the Imagination was able to represent simultaneously a more comprehensive system ; and thus the several parts being regarded and valued only as conducive to the general result,—these parts never obtained that individual importance, which would have fallen to them had they been only created and only considered for themselves. Now this power of representing to the mind a complex system in all its bearings, is not less requisite to the philosopher than to the poet, though the representation be different in kind ; and the nature of the philosophic representations, as not concrete and palpable like the poetical, supposes a more arduous operation, and, therefore, even a more vigorous faculty. But Imagination, in the one case and in the other, requires in proportion to its own power a powerful intellect; for imagination is not poetry nor philosophy, but only the condition of the one and of the other.

But to speak now of the Errors which arise from the disproportion between the Imagination and the Judgment ; they originate either in the weakness, or in the inordinate strength, of the former.

Errors which arise from the disproportion between Imagination and Judgment.

Those arising from the weakness of Imagination.

In regard to the errors which arise from the imbecility of the Representative Faculty, it is not difficult to conceive how this imbecility may become a cause of erroneous judgment. The Elaborative Faculty, in order to judge, requires an object, —requires certain differences to be given. Now, if the imagination be weak and languid, the objects represented by it will be given in such confusion and obscurity, that their differences are either null or evanescent, and judgment thus rendered either impossible, or possible only with the probability of error. In these circumstances, to secure itself from failure, the intellect must not attempt to rise above the actual presentations of sense ; it must not attempt any ideal analysis or synthesis,—it must abandon all free and self-active elaboration, and all hope of a successful cultivation of knowledge.

Again, in regard to the opposite errors, those arising from the disproportioned vivacity of imagination,

<small>From its disproportionate vivacity.</small>

—these are equally apparent. In this case the renewed or newly-modified representations make an equal impression on the mind as the original presentations, and are, consequently, liable to be mistaken for these. Even during the perception of real objects, a too lively imagination mingles itself with the observation, which it thus corrupts and falsifies. Thus arises what is logically called the *vitium subreptionis*. This is frequently seen in those pretended observations made by theorists in support of their hypotheses, in which, if even the possibility be left for imagination to interfere, imagination is sure to fill up all that the senses may leave vacant. In this case the observers are at once dupes and deceivers, in the words of Tacitus, "*Fingunt simul creduntque.*"

In regard to the remedies for these defects of the Representative Faculty;—in the former case, the only alleviation that can be proposed for a feeble imagination, is to animate it by the contemplation and study of those works of art which are the products of a strong Phantasy, and which tend to awaken in the student a corresponding energy of that faculty. On the other hand, a too powerful imagination is to be quelled and regulated by abstract thinking, and the study of philosophical, perhaps of mathematical, science.

Remedies for these defects of the Imagination.

The faculty which next follows, is the Elaborative Faculty, Comparison, or the Faculty of Relations. This is the Understanding, in its three functions of Conception, Judgment, and Reasoning. On this faculty take the following paragraph.

¶ XIII. The Affections and the Lower Cognitive Faculties afford the sources and occasions of error ; but it is the Elaborative Faculty, Understanding, Comparison, or Judgment, which truly errs. This faculty does not, however, err from strength or over-activity, but from inaction ; and this inaction arises either from natural weakness, from want of exercise, or from the impotence of attention.

Par. XIII. 5. Elaborative Faculty,— as a source of Error.

I formerly observed that error does not lie in the conditions of our higher faculties themselves, and that these faculties are not, by their own laws, determined to false judgments or conclusions :

Explication. Error does not lie in the conditions of our Higher Faculties, but is possible in the application of the laws of those faculties to determinate cases.

"*Nam neque decipitur ratio, nec decipit unquam.*" If these were otherwise, all knowledge would be impossible,—the root of our nature would be a lie. " But in the application of the laws of our higher faculties to determinate cases, many errors are possible; and these errors may actually be occasioned by a variety of circumstances. Thus, it is a law of our intelligence, that no event, no phenomenon, can be thought as absolutely beginning to be; we cannot but think that all its constituent elements had a virtual existence prior to their concurrence, to necessitate its manifestation to us; we are thus unable to accord to it more than a relative commencement, in other words, we are constrained to look upon it as the effect of antecedent causes. Now though the law itself of our intelligence—that a cause there is for every event—be altogether exempt from error, yet in the application of this law to individual cases, that is, in the attribution of determinate causes to determinate effects, we are easily liable to go wrong. For we do not know, except from experience and induction, what particular antecedents are the causes of particular consequents; and if our knowledge of this relation be imperfectly generalized, or if we extend it by a false analogy to cases not included within our observation, error is the inevitable consequence. But in all this there is no fault, no failure, of intelligence, there is only a deficiency,—a deficiency in the activity of intelligence, while the Will determines us to a decision before the Understanding has become fully conscious of certainty. The defective action of the Understanding may arise from three causes. In the first place, the Faculty of Judgment may by nature be too feeble. This is the case in idiots and weak persons. In the second place, though not by nature incompetent to judge, the intellect may be without the necessary experience,—may not possess the grounds on which a correct

<small>Defective action of the Understanding may arise from three causes.
(*a*) Natural feebleness. (*b*) Want of necessary experience. (*c*) Incompetency of attention.</small>

judgment must be founded. In the third place,—and this is the most frequent cause of error,—the failure of the understanding is from the incompetency of that act of will which is called *Attention*. Attention is the voluntary direction of the mind upon an object, with the intention of fully apprehending it. The cognitive energy is thus, as it were, concentrated upon a single point. We, therefore, say that the mind collects itself, when it begins to be attentive; on the contrary, that it is distracted, when its attention is not turned upon an object as it ought to be. This fixing— this concentration, of the mind upon an object can only be carried to a certain degree, and continued for a certain time. This degree and this continuance are both dependent upon bodily circumstances; and they are also frequently interrupted or suspended by the intrusion of certain collateral objects, which are forced upon the mind, either from without, by a strong and sudden impression upon the senses, or from within, through the influence of Association; and these, when once obtruded, gradually or at once divert the attention from the original and principal object. If we are not sufficiently attentive, or if the effort which accompanies the concentration of the mind upon a single object be irksome, there arises hurry and thoughtlessness in judging, inasmuch as we judge either before we have fully sought out the grounds on which our decision ought to proceed, or have competently examined their validity and effect. It is hence manifest that a multitude of errors is the inevitable consequence.

In regard to the Regulative Faculty,—Common Sense,—Intelligence,—νοῦς,—this is not in itself a source of error. Errors may, however, arise either from overlooking the laws or necessary principles which it does contain; or by attributing to it, as necessary and original data, what are only contingent generalizations from experience, and, consequently, make no part of its complement of native truths. But these errors, it is evident, are not to be attributed to the Regulating Faculty itself, which is only a place or source of principles, but to the imperfect operations of the Understanding and Self-consciousness, in not properly observing and sifting the phenomena which it reveals.

6. Regulative Faculty,—not properly a source of Error.

Besides these sources of Error, which immediately originate in the several powers and faculties of mind, there are others of a remoter origin arising from the different habits which are determined by the differences of sex, of age, of bodily constitution, of education, of rank, of fortune, of profession, of intellectual pursuit. Of these, however, it is impossible at present to attempt an analysis; and I shall only endeavor to afford you a few specimens, and to refer you for information in regard to the others to the best sources.

Remote sources of Error in the different habits determinated by sex, age, bodily constitution, education, etc.

Intellectual pursuits or favorite studies, inasmuch as these determine the mind to a one-sided cultivation, that is, to the neglect of some, and to the disproportioned development of other, of its faculties, are among the most remarkable causes of error. This partial or one-sided cultivation is exemplified in three different phases. The first of these is shown in the exclusive cultivation of the powers of Observation, to the neglect of the higher faculties of the Understanding. Of this type are your men of physical science. In this department of

Selected examples of these.
A one-sided cultivation of the intellectual powers.
This exemplified in three different phases. Exclusive cultivation. 1. Of the powers of Observation.

knowledge there is chiefly demanded a patient habit of attention to details, in order to detect phenomena, and, these discovered, their generalization is usually so easy that there is little exercise afforded to the higher energies of Judgment and Reasoning. It was Bacon's boast, that Induction, as applied to nature, would equalize all talents, level the aristocracy of genius, accomplish marvels by coöperation and method, and leave little to be done by the force of individual intellects. This boast has been fulfilled. Science has, by the Inductive Process, been brought down to minds, who previously would have been incompetent for its cultivation, and physical knowledge now usefully occupies many who would otherwise have been without any rational pursuit. But the exclusive devotion to such studies, if not combined with higher and graver speculations, tends to wean the student from the more vigorous efforts of mind, which, though unamusing and even irksome at the commencement, tend, however, to invigorate his nobler powers, and to prepare him for the final fruition of the highest happiness of his intellectual nature.

A partial cultivation of the intellect, opposite to this, is given in the exclusive cultivation of Meta-
2. Of Metaphysics.
3. Of Mathematics.
Stewart referred to. physics and of Mathematics. On this subject I may refer you to some observations of Mr. Stewart, in two chapters entitled *The Metaphysician,* and *The Mathematician,* in the third volume of his *Elements of the Philosophy of the Human Mind,*—chapters distinguished equally by their candor and their depth of observation. On this subject Mr. Stewart's authority is of the highest, inasmuch as he was distinguished in both the departments of knowledge, the tendency of which he so well develops.

7*

LECTURE V.—MODIFIED STOICHEIOLOGY.

SECTION II.—ERROR.—ITS CAUSES AND REMEDIES.

C.—LANGUAGE.—D.—OBJECTS OF KNOWLEDGE.

IN my last Lecture, I concluded the survey of the Errors which have their origin in the conditions and circumstances of the several Cognitive Faculties, and now proceed to that source of false judgment which lies in the imperfection of the Instrument of thought and Communication,—I mean Language.

<small>III. Language,—as a source of Error.</small>

Much controversy has arisen in regard to the question,— Has man invented Language? But the differences of opinion have in a great measure arisen from the ambiguity or complexity of the terms, in which the problem has been stated. By *language* we may mean either the power which man possesses of associating his thought with signs, or the particular systems of signs with which different portions of mankind have actually so associated their thoughts.

<small>Has man invented Language? Ambiguity of the question.</small>

Taking *language* in the former sense, it is a natural faculty, an original tendency of mind, and, in this view, man has no more invented language than he has invented thought. In fact, the power of thought and the power of language are equally entitled to be considered as elementary qualities of intelligence; for while they are so different that they cannot be identified, they are still so reciprocally necessary that the one cannot exist without the other. It is true, indeed, that presentations and representations of given individual objects might have taken place, although there were no signs with which they were mentally connected, and by which they could be overtly expressed; but all complex and factitious constructions out of these given individual objects, in other words, all notions, concepts, general ideas, or thoughts proper, would have been impossible without an association to certain signs, by which their scattered elements might be combined in unity, and their vague and evanescent existence obtain a kind of definite and fixed and palpable reality. Speech and cogitation are thus the relative conditions of each other's activity, and both concur to the accomplishment of the same joint result. The Faculty of Thinking—the Faculty of forming General Notions—being given, this necessarily tends to energy, but the energy of thinking depends upon the coäctivity of the Faculty of Speech, which itself tends equally to energy. These faculties,—these tendencies,— these energies, thus coëxist and have alway coëxisted; and the result of their combined action is thought in language, and language in thought. So much for the origin of Language, considered in general as a faculty.

In what sense Language is natural to man.

But, though the Faculty of Speech be natural and necessary, that its manifestations are, to a certain extent, contingent and artificial, is evident from the simple fact, that there are more than a single language actually spoken. It may, therefore, be asked— Was the first language, actually spoken, the invention of man, or an inspiration of the Deity? The latter hypothesis cuts, but does not loose the knot. It declares that ordinary causes and the laws of nature are insufficient to explain the phenomenon, but it does not prove this insufficiency; it thus violates the rule of Parcimony, by postulating a second and hypothetical cause to explain an effect, which it is not shown cannot be accounted for without this violent assumption. The first and greatest difficulty in the question is thus:—It is necessary to think in order to invent a language, and the invention of a language is necessary in order to think; for we cannot think without notions, and notions are only fixed by words. This can only be solved, as I have said, by the natural attraction between thought and speech,— by their secret affinity, which is such that they suggest and, *pari passu*, accompany each other. And in regard to the question,—Why, if speech be a natural faculty, it does not manifest itself like other natural principles in a uniform manner,—it may be answered that the Faculty of Speech is controlled and modified in its exercise by external circumstances, in consequence of which, though its exertion be natural and necessary, and, therefore, identical in all men, the special forms of its exertion are in a great degree, con-

Marginalia:
- Was the first language, actually spoken, the invention of man, or an inspiration of the Deity?
- The latter hypothesis considered.
- Difficulty of the question.

ventional and contingent, and, therefore, different among different portions of mankind.

Considered on one side, languages are the results of our intelligence and its immutable laws. In consequence of this, they exhibit in their progress and development resemblances and common characters which allow us to compare and to recall them to certain primitive and essential forms,—to evolve a system of Universal Grammar. Considered on another side, each language is the offspring of particular wants, of special circumstances, physical and moral, and of chance. Hence it is that every language has particular forms as it has peculiar words. Language thus bears the impress of human intelligence only in its general outlines. There is, therefore, to be found reason and philosophy in all languages, but we should be wrong in believing that reason and philosophy have, in any language, determined everything. No tongue, how perfect soever it may appear, is a complete and perfect instrument of human thought. From its very conditions every language must be imperfect. The human memory can only compass a limited complement of words, but the data of sense, and still more the combinations of the understanding, are wholly unlimited in number. No language can, therefore, be adequate to the ends for which it exists; all are imperfect, but some are far less incompetent instruments than others.

Language has a general and a special character.

No language is a perfect instrument of thought.

From what has now been said, you will be prepared to find in Language one of the principal sources of Error; but before I go on to consider the particular modes in which the Imperfections of Language are the causes of false judgments,—I shall comprise the general doctrine in the following paragraph :

<small>Par. XIV. Language,—as a source of Error.</small>

¶ XIV. As the human mind necessarily requires the aid of signs to elaborate, to fix, and to communicate its notions, and as Articulate Sounds are the species of signs which most effectually afford this aid, Speech is, therefore, an indispensable instrument in the higher functions of thought and knowledge. But as speech is a necessary, but not a perfect, instrument, its imperfection must react upon the mind. For the Multitude of Languages, the Difficulty of their Acquisition, their necessary Inadequacy, and the consequent Ambiguity of Words, both singly and in combination,—these are all copious sources of Illusion and Error.

<small>Explication. Signs necessary for the internal operation of Thought.</small>

We have already sufficiently considered the reason why thought is dependent upon some system of signs or symbols both for its internal perfection and external expression. The analyses and syntheses,—the decompositions and compositions,—in a word, the elaborations, performed by the Understanding upon the objects presented by External Perception and Self-Consciousness, and represented by Imagination,—these operations are faint and fugitive, and would have no existence, even for the conscious mind, beyond the moment of present consciousness, were we not able to connect, to ratify, and to fix them, by giving to their parts (which would otherwise immediately fall asunder) a permanent unity, by associating them with a sensible symbol, which we may always recall at pleasure, and which, when recalled, recalls along with it the characters which concur in constituting a notion or factitious object of intelligence. So far signs are necessary for the internal operation of thought itself. But for the communication of thought from one mind to another, signs are equally indispensable. For in itself thought is known,—thought it is knowable, only to the thinking mind itself; and were we not enabled to connect certain complements of thought to certain sensible symbols, and by their means to suggest in other minds those complements of thought of which we were conscious in ourselves, we should never be able to communicate to others what engaged our interest, and man would remain for man, if an intelligence at all, a mere isolated intelligence.

And for the communication of Thought.

In regard to the question,—What may these sensible symbols be, by which we are to compass such memorable effects,—it is needless to show that mien and gesture, which, to a certain extent, afford a kind of natural expression, are altogether inadequate to the double purpose of thought and communication, which it is here required to accomplish. This double purpose can be effected only by symbols, which express, through intonations of the voice, what is passing in the mind. These vocal intonations are either inarticulate or articulate. The former are mere sounds or cries; and, as such, an expression of the feelings of which the lower animals are also capable. The latter constitute words, and these, as the expression of thoughts or notions, constitute Language Proper or Speech. Speech, as we have said, as the instrument of elaborating, fixing, and communicating our

Intonations of the voice the only adequate sensible symbols of thought and its communication.
These inarticulate and articulate.
The latter constitute Language Proper.
How Language is a source of Error.

thoughts, is a principal mean of knowledge, and even the indispensable condition on which depends the exercise of our higher cognitive faculties. But, at the same time, in consequence of this very dependence of thought upon language, inasmuch as language is itself not perfect, the understanding is not only restrained in its operations, and its higher development, consequently, checked, but many occasions are given of positive error. For, to say nothing of the impediment presented to the free communication of thought by the multitude of tongues into which human language is divided, in consequence of which all speech beyond their mother-tongue is incomprehensible to those who do not make a study of other languages,—even the accurate learning of a single language is attended with such difficulties, that perhaps there never yet has been an individual who was thoroughly acquainted with all the words and modes of verbal combination in any single language,—his mother-tongue even not excepted. But the circumstance of principal importance is, that how copious and expressive soever it may be, no language is competent adequately to denote all possible notions, and all possible relations of notions, and from this necessary poverty of language in all its different degrees, a certain inevitable ambiguity arises, both in the employment of single words and of words in mutual connection.

<small>The ambiguity of words the principal source of error originating in Language.</small>

As this is the principal source of the error originating in Language, it will be proper to be a little more explicit. And here it is expedient to take into account two circumstances, which mutually affect each other. The first is, that as the vocabulary of every language is neces-

<small>Two circumstances under this head, which mutually affect each other.</small>

sarily finite, it is necessarily disproportioned to the multiplicity, not to say infinity, of thought; and the second, that the complement of words in any given language has been always filled up with terms significant of objects and relations of the external world, before the want was experienced of words to express the objects and relations of the internal.

From the first of these circumstances, considered exclusively and by itself, it is manifest that one of two alternatives must take place. Either the words of a language must each designate only a single notion,—a single fasciculus of thought,—the multitude of notions not designated being allowed to perish, never obtaining more than a momentary existence in the mind of the individual; or the words of a language must each be employed to denote a plurality of concepts. In the former case, a small amount of thought would be expressed, but that precisely and without ambiguity; in the latter, a large amount of thought would be expressed, but that vaguely and equivocally. Of these alternatives (each of which has thus its advantages and disadvantages), the latter is the one which has universally been preferred; and, accordingly, all languages by the same word express a multitude of thoughts, more or less differing from each other. Now, what is the consequence of this? It is plain that if a word has more than a single meaning attached to it, when it is employed it cannot of itself directly and peremptorily suggest any definite thought;—all that it can do is vaguely and hypothetically to suggest a variety of different notions; and we are obliged from the consideration of the context,—of the tenor,—of the general analogy, of the discourse, to surmise,

The vocabulary of every language necessarily finite. Consequences of this.

with greater or less assurance, with greater or less precision, what particular bundle of characters it was intended to convey. Words, in fact, as languages are constituted, do nothing more than suggest, are nothing more than hints; hints, likewise, which leave the principal part of the process of interpretation to be performed by the mind of the hearer. In this respect, the effect of words resembles the effect of an outline or shade of a countenance with which we are familiar. In both cases, the mind is stimulated to fill up what is only hinted or pointed at. Thus it is that the function of language is not so much to infuse knowledge from one intelligence to another, as to bring two minds into the same train of thinking, and to confine them to the same track. In this procedure what is chiefly wonderful, is the rapidity with which the mind compares the word with its correlations, and in general, without the slightest effort, decides which among its various meanings is the one which it is here intended to convey. But how marvellous soever be the ease and velocity of this process of selection, it cannot always be performed with equal certainty. Words are often employed with a plurality of meanings; several of which may quadrate, or be supposed to quadrate, with the general tenor of the discourse. Error is thus possible; and it is also probable, if we have any prepossession in favor of one interpretation rather than of another. So copious a source of error is the ambiguity of language, that a very large proportion of human controversy has been concerning the sense in which certain terms should be understood; and many disputes have even been fiercely waged, in consequence of the disputants being unaware that they agreed in opinion, and only differed in the meaning they attached

Words are merely hints to the mind.

to the words in which that opinion was expressed. On this subject I may refer you to the very amusing and very instructive treatise of Werenfelsius, entitled *De Logomachiis Eruditorum.*

In regard to a remedy for this description of error,—this lies exclusively in a thorough study of the language employed in the communication of knowledge, and in an acquaintance with the rules of Criticism and Interpretation. The study of languages, when rationally pursued, is not so unimportant as many fondly conceive; for misconceptions most frequently arise solely from an ignorance of words; and every language may, in a certain sort, be viewed as a commentary upon Logic, inasmuch as every language, in like manner, mirrors in itself the laws of thought.

<small>Remedy for error arising from Language.</small>

In reference to the rules of Criticism and Interpretation, —these especially should be familiar to those who make a study of the writings of ancient authors, as these writings have descended to us often in a very mutilated state, and are composed in languages which are now dead. How many theological errors, for example, have only arisen because the divines were either ignorant of the principles of Criticism and Hermeneutic, or did not properly apply them! Doctrines originating in a corrupted lection, or in a figurative expression, have thus arisen and been keenly defended. Such errors are best combated by philological weapons; for these pull them up along with their roots.

A thorough knowledge of languages in general accustoms the mind not to remain satisfied with the husk, but to penetrate in, even to the kernel. With this knowledge we shall not so easily imagine that we understand a system, when we only possess the language in which it is expressed; we shall not conceive that we truly reason, when we only employ certain empty words and formulæ; we shall not betray ourselves into unusual and obscure expressions, under which our meaning may be easily mistaken; finally, we shall not dispute with others about words, when we are in fact at one with them in regard to things. So much for the errors which originate in Language.

As to the last source of Error which I enumerated,—the Objects themselves of our knowledge,—it is hardly necessary to say anything. It is evident that some matters are obscure and abstruse, while others are clear and palpable; and that, consequently, the probability of error is greater in some studies than it is in others. But as it is impossible to deliver any special rules for these cases, different from those which are given for the Acquisition of Knowledge in general, concerning which we are soon to speak,—this source of error may be, therefore, passed over in silence.

IV. Source of Error, —the Objects of our Knowledge.

We have now thus finished the consideration of the various Sources of Error, and—

¶ XV. The following rules may be given, as the results of the foregoing discussion, touching the Causes and Remedies of our False Judgments.

Par. XV. Rules touching the Causes and Remedies of our False Judgments.

1°, Endeavor as far as possible to obtain a clear and thorough insight into the laws of the Understanding, and of the Mental Faculties in general. Study Logic and Psychology.

2°, Assiduously exercise your mind in the application of these laws. Learn to think methodically.

3°, Concentrate your attention in the act of Thinking; and principally employ the seasons when the Intellect is alert, the Passions slumbering, and no external causes of distraction at work.

4°, Carefully eliminate all foreign interests from the objects of your enquiry, and allow yourselves to be actuated by the interest of Truth alone.

5°, Contrast your various convictions, your past and present judgments, with each other; and admit no conclusion as certain, until it has been once and again thoroughly examined, and its correctness ascertained.

6°, Collate your own persuasions with those of others; attentively listen to and weigh, without prepossession, the judgments formed by others of the opinions which you yourselves maintain.

LECTURE VI.—MODIFIED METHODOLOGY.

SECTION I.—OF THE ACQUISITION OF KNOWLEDGE.

I. EXPERIENCE.—A. PERSONAL:—OBSERVATION—INDUCTION AND ANALOGY.

Means by which our knowledge obtains the character of Perfection, viz., the Acquisition and the Communication of Knowledge.

IN our last Lecture, having concluded the Second Department of Concrete Logic,—that which treats of the Causes of Error, we now enter upon the Third part of Concrete or Modified Logic,—that which considers the Means by which our Knowledge obtains the character of Perfection. These means may, in general, be regarded as two,— the Acquisition and the Communication of knowledge,—and these two means we shall, accordingly, consider consecutively and apart.

The acquisition of Knowledge.

In regard to the Acquisition of Knowledge,—we must consider this by reference to the different kinds of knowledge of which the human intellect is capable. And this, viewed in its greatest universality, is of two species.

Human Knowledge of two kinds.

Human knowledge, I say, viewed in its greatest universality, is of two kinds. For either it is one of which the objects are given as contingent phænomena, or one in which the objects are given as necessary facts or laws. In the former case, the cognitions are called *empirical, experiential*, or *of experience ;* in the latter, *pure, intuitive, rational*, or *of reason*, also *of common sense.* These two kinds of knowledge are, likewise, severally denominated *cognitions a posteriori* and *cognitions a priori.* The distinction of these two species of cognitions consists properly in this,—that the former are solely derived from the Presentations of Sense, External and Internal; whereas the latter, though first manifested on the occasion of such Presentations, are not, however, mere products of Sense ; on the contrary, they are laws, principles, forms, notions, or by whatever name they may be called, native and original to the mind, that is, founded in, or constituting the very nature of, Intelligence ; and, accordingly, out of the mind itself they must be developed, and not sought for and acquired as foreign and accidental acquisitions. As the Presentative Faculties inform us only of what exists and what happens, that is, only of facts and events,—such empirical knowledge constitutes no necessary and universal judgment ; all, in this case, is contingent and particular, for even our generalized knowledge has only a relative and precarious universality. The cognitions, on the other hand, which are given as Laws of Mind, are, at once and in themselves, universal and necessary. We cannot but think them, if we think at all. The doctrine, therefore, of the Acquisition of Knowledge, must consist of two parts,—the first treating of the acquisition of knowledge through the data of experience, the second, of the acquisition of knowledge through the data of Intelligence.

<small>Doctrine of the Acquisition of Knowledge consists of two parts.</small>

In regard to the first of these sources, viz., Experience,—
this is either our own experience or the
experience of others, and in either case
it is for us a mean of knowledge. It is
manifest that the knowledge we acquire
through our personal experience, is far superior in degree to
that which we obtain through the experience of other men;
inasmuch as our knowledge of an object, in the former case,
is far clearer and more distinct, far more complete and
lively, than in the latter; while at the same time the latter
also affords us a far inferior conviction of the correctness
and certainty of the cognition than the former. On the other
hand, foreign is far superior to our proper experience in
this,—that it is much more comprehensive, and that, without this, man would be deprived of those branches of
knowledge which are to him of the most indispensable
importance. Now, as the principal distinction of experience
is thus into our own experience and into the experience of
others, we must consider it more closely in this two-fold
relation. First, then, of our Personal Experience.

<small>I. The doctrine of Experience. Experience of two kinds.</small>

Experience necessarily supposes, as its primary condition,
certain presentations by the faculties of External or of
Internal Perception, and is, therefore, of
two kinds, according as it is conversant
about the objects of the one of these
faculties, or the objects of the other. But
the presentation of a fact of the external or of the
internal world is not at once an experience. To this
there is required a continued series of such presentations, a comparison of these together, a mental separation
of the different, a mental combination of the similar, and
it, therefore, over and above the operation of the Presenta-

<small>1. Personal Experience.</small>

tive Faculties, requires the coöperation of the Retentive, the Reproductive, the Representative, and the Elaborative Faculties. In regard to Experience, as the first means by which we acquire knowledge through the legitimate use and application of our Cognitive Faculties, I give you the following paragraph :

¶ XVI. The First Mean towards the Acquisition of Knowledge is *Experience* (*experi-*

Par. XVI. Experience; what,— in general.

entia, ἐμπειρία). Experience may be, rudely and generally, described as the apprehension of the phænomena of the outer world, presented by the Faculty of External Perception, and of the phænomena of the inner world, presented by the Faculty of Self-consciousness ;—these phænomena being retained in Memory, ready for Reproduction and Representation, being also arranged into order by the Understanding.

This paragraph, you will remark, affords only a preliminary view of the general conditions of Experience. In the first place, it is evident, that without the Presentative, or, as they may with equal propriety be called, the Acquisitive, Faculties of Perception, External and Internal, no experience would be possible. But these faculties, though affording the fundamental condition of knowledge, do not of themselves make up experience. There is, moreover, required of the phænomena or appearances the accumulation and retention, the reproduction and representation. Memory, Reminiscence, and Imagination must, therefore, also coöperate. Finally, unless the phænomena be compared together, and be arranged into classes, according to their similarities and differences, it is evident that no judgments,—no conclusions,

Explication.

can be formed concerning them; but without a judgment knowledge is impossible; and as experience is a knowledge, consequently experience is impossible. The Understanding or Elaborative Faculty must, therefore, likewise coöperate. Manilius has well expressed the nature of experience in the following lines.

> "*Per varios usus artem experientia fecit,*
> *Exemplo monstrante viam.*"

And Afranius in the others:

> "*Usus me genuit, mater peperit Memoria;*
> *Sophiam vocant me Graii, vos Sapientiam.*"

<small>Common and Scientific Experience.</small>

Our own observation, be it external or internal, is either with, or without, intention; and it consists either of a series of Presentations alone, or Abstraction and Reflection supervene, so that the presentations obtain that completion and system which they do not of themselves possess. In the former case, the experience may be called an *Unlearned* or *Common;* in the latter, a *Learned* or *Scientific Experience.* Intentional and reflective experience is called *Observation.*

<small>Observation—what. Of two kinds,—Observation Proper, and Experiment.</small>

Observation is of two kinds; for either the objects which it considers remain unchanged, or, previous to its application, they are made to undergo certain arbitrary changes, or are placed in certain factitious relations. In the latter case, the observation contains the specific name of *Experiment.* Observation and experiment do not, therefore, constitute opposite or two different procedures,—the latter is, in propriety, only a certain subordinate modification of the former; for, while observation may accomplish its end without experiment, experiment without observation is impossible. Observation and experiment are manifestly exclusively competent upon the objects of our empirical knowledge ; and they coöperate, equally and in like manner, to the progress of that knowledge, partly by establishing, partly by correcting, partly by amplifying it. Under observation, therefore, is not to be understood a common or unlearned experience, which obtrudes itself upon every one endowed with the ordinary faculties of Sense and Understanding, but an intentional and continued application of the faculties of Perception, combined with an abstractive and reflective attention to an object or class of objects, a more accurate knowledge of which, it is proposed, by the observation, to accomplish. But in order that the observation should accomplish this end,—more especially when the objects are numerous and a systematic complement of cognitions is the end proposed,—

<small>Præcognita of Observation.</small> it is necessary that we should know certain præcognita,—1°, What we ought to observe; 2°, How we ought to observe; and 3°, By what means are the data of observation to be reduced to system. The first of these concerns the Object ; the second, the Procedure ; the third, the scientific Completion of the observations. It is proper to make some general observations in regard to these, in their order ; and first, of the Object of observation,—the *what* we ought to observe.

The Object of Observation can only be some given and determined phænomenon, and this phæno-
<small>First,—The Object of Observation. This fourfold.</small> menon either an external or an internal. Through observation, whether external or internal, there are four several cognitions which we propose to compass, viz., to ascertain—1°, What

the Phænomena themselves are; 2°, What are the Conditions of their Reality; 3°, What are the Causes of their Existence; 4°, What is the Order of their Consecution.

In regard to what the phænomena themselves are *(quid sint)*, that is, in regard to what constitutes their peculiar nature,—this, it is evident, must be the primary matter of consideration, it being always supposed that the fact (the *an sit)* of the phænomenon itself has been established. To this there is required, above all, a clear and distinct Presentation or Representation of the object. In order to obtain this, it behooves us to analyze,—to dismember,—the constituent parts of the object, and to take into proximate account those characters which constitute the object, that is, which make it to be what it is, and nothing but what it is. This being performed, we must proceed to compare it with other objects, and with those especially which bear to it the strongest similarity, taking accurate note always of those points in which they reciprocally resemble and in which they reciprocally disagree.

1°, What the Phænomena are.

In their individual peculiarities and contrasts.

But it is not enough to consider the several phænomena in their individual peculiarities and contrasts,—in what they are, and in what they are not,—it is also requisite to bring them under determinate genera and species. To this end we must, having obtained (as previously prescribed) a clear and distinct knowledge of the several phænomena in their essential similarities and differences, look away or abstract from the latter,—the differences, and comprehend the former,—the similarities, in a compendious and characteristic notion, under an appropriate name.

As under determinate genera and species.

When the distinctive peculiarities of the phænomena have been thus definitely recognized, the second question emerges,—What are the Conditions of their Reality. These conditions are commonly called *Requisites*, and under *requisite* we must understand all that must have preceded, before the phænomena could follow. In order to discover the requisites, we take a number of analogous cases, or cases similar in kind, and inquire what are the circumstances under which the phænomena always arises, if it does arise, and what are the circumstances under which it never arises; and then, after a competent observation of individual cases, we construct the general judgment, that the phænomenon never occurs unless this or that other phænomenon has preceded, or at least accompanied, it. Here, however, it must be noticed, that nothing can be viewed as a requisite which admits of any, even the smallest, exception.

2°, What the Conditions of their Reality.

The requisite conditions being discovered, the third question arises,—What are the Causes of the Phænomena. According to the current doctrine, the *causes* of phænomena are not to be confounded with their *requisites;* for although a phænomenon no more occurs without its requisite than without its cause, still, the requisite being given, the phænomenon does not necessarily follow, and, indeed, very frequently does not ensue. On the contrary, if the cause occurs, the phænomenon must occur also. In other words, the requisite or condition is that without which the phænomenon never is; the cause, on the other hand, is that through which it always is. Thus an emotion of pity never arises without a knowledge of the misfortune of another; but so little does this knowledge necessitate that emotion,

3°, What the Causes of the Phænomena.

that its opposite, a feeling of rejoicing, complacency, at such suffering may ensue; whereas the knowledge of another's misfortune must be followed by a sentiment of pity, if we are predisposed in favor of the person to whom the misfortune has occurred. In this view, the knowledge of another's misfortune is only a requisite; whereas our favorable predisposition constitutes the cause. It must, however, be admitted, that in different relations one and the same circumstance may be both requisite and cause; and, in point of fact, it would be more correct to consider the cause as the whole sum of antecedents, without which the phænomenon never does take place, and with which it always must. What are commonly called *requisites*, are thus, in truth, only partial causes; what are called *causes*, only proximate requisites.

In the fourth place, having ascertained the essential qualities,—the Conditions and the Causes of phænomena,—a final question emerges,—What is the Order in which they are manifested? and this being ascertained, the observation has accomplished its end. This question applies either to a phænomenon considered in itself, or to a phænomenon considered in relation to others. In relation to itself, the question concerns only the time of its origin, of its continuance, and of its termination; in relation to others, it concerns the reciprocal consecution in which the several phænomena appear.

<small>4°, What the Order of their Consecution.</small>

We now go on to the second Præcognitum,—the Manner of Observation,—How we are to observe. What we have hitherto spoken of—the Object—can be known only in one way,—the way of Scientific Observation. It therefore remains to

<small>Second,—The Manner of Observation.</small>

be asked,—How must the observation be instituted, so as to afford us a satisfactory result in regard to all the four sides on which it behooves an object to be observed? In the first place, as preliminary to observa-

1°, Proper state of the observing mind.

tion, it is required that the observing mind be tranquil and composed, be exempt from prejudice, partiality, and prepossession, and be actuated by no other interest than the discovery of truth. Tranquility and composure of mind are of peculiar importance in our observation of the phænomena of the internal world; for these phænomena are not, like those of the external, perceptible by sense, enclosed in space, continuous and divisible; and they follow each other in such numbers, and with such a rapidity, that they are at best observable with difficulty, often losing even their existence by the interference of the observing,—the reflective energy, itself. But that the observation should be always conducted in the calm and collected state of mind required to purify this condition, we must be careful to obtain, more and more, a mastery over the Attention, so as to turn it with full force upon a single aspect of the phænomena, and, consequently, to abstract it altogether from every other. Its proper function is to contemplate the objects of observation tranquilly, continuously, and without anxiety for the result; and this, likewise, without too intense an activity or too vigorous an application of its forces. But the observation and concomitant energy of attention will be without result, unless we previously well consider what precise object or objects we are now to observe. Nor will our experience obtain an answer to the question proposed for it to solve, unless that question be of such a nature as will animate the observing faculties by some stimulus, and give them a determinate direction. Where this is not the case, attention does not effect anything, nay, it does not operate at all. On this account such psychological questions as the following: What takes place in the process of Self-consciousness,—of Perception,—of Vision, —of Hearing,—of Imagination, etc.,—cannot be answered, as thus absolutely stated, that is, without reference to some determinate object. But if I propose the problem,—What takes place when I see this or that object, or better still, when I see this table,—the attention is stimulated and directed, and even a child can give responses, which, if properly illustrated and explained, will afford a solution to the problem. If, therefore, the question upon the object of observation be too vague and general, so that the attention is not suitably excited and applied,—this question must be divided and subdivided into others more particular, and this process must be continued until we reach a question which affords the requisite conditions. We should, therefore, determine as closely as possible the object itself, and the phases in which we wish to observe it, separate from it all foreign or adventitious parts, resolve every question into its constituent elements, enunciate each of these as specially as possible, and never couch it in vague and general expressions. But here we must at the same time take care that the object be not so torn and mangled that the attention feels no longer any attraction to the several parts, or that the several parts can no longer be viewed in their natural connection. So much it is possible to say in general, touching the Manner in which observation ought to be carried on; what may further be added under this head, depends upon the particular nature of the objects to be observed.

2°, Conditions of the question to be determined by the observation.

In this manner, then, must we proceed, until all has been accomplished which the problem, to be answered by the observation, pointed out. When the observation is concluded, an accurate record or notation of what has been observed is of use, in order to enable us to supply what is found wanting in our subsequent observation. If we have accumulated a considerable apparatus of results, in relation to the object we observe, it is proper to take a survey of these; from what is found defective, new questions must be evolved, and an answer to these sought out through new observations. When the inquiry has attained its issue, a tabular view of all the observations made upon the subject is convenient, to afford a conspectus of the whole, and as an aid to the memory. But how (and this is the Third Precognition) individual observations are to be built up into a systematic whole, is to be sought for partly from the nature of science in general, partly from the nature of the particular empirical science for the constitution of which the observation is applied. Nor is what is thus sought difficult to find. It is at once evident, that a synthetic arrangement is least applicable in the empirical sciences. For, anterior to observation, the object is absolutely unknown; and it is only through observation that it becomes a matter of science. We can, therefore, only go to work in a problematic or interrogative manner, and it is impossible to commence by assertory propositions, of which we afterwards lead the demonstration. We must, therefore, determine the objects on all sides, in so far as observation is competent to this; we must analyze every question into its subordinate questions, and each of these must find its answer in observation. The systematic order is thus given

Third,—The means by which the data of Observation are to be reduced to system.

8*

naturally and of itself; and in this procedure it is impossible that it should not be given. But for a comprehensive and all-sided system of empirical knowledge, it is not sufficient to possess the whole data of observation, to have collected these together, and to have arranged them according to some external principle; it is, likewise, requisite that we have a thorough-going principle of explanation, even though this explanation be impossible in the way of observation, and a power of judging of the data, according to universal laws, although these universal laws may not be discovered by experience alone. These two ends are accomplished by different means. The former we compass by the aid of Hypothesis, the latter, by the aid of Induction and Analogy. Of these in detail. In regard to Hypothesis, I give you the following paragraph.

¶ XVII. When a phænomenon is presented, which can be explained by no principle afforded through Experience, we feel discontented and uneasy; and there arises an effort to discover some cause which may, at least provisorily, account for the outstanding phænomenon; and this cause is finally recognized as valid and true, if, through it, the given phænomenon is found to obtain a full and perfect explanation. The judgment in which a phænomenon is referred to such a problematic cause, is called an *Hypothesis*.

<small>Par. XVII. Hypothesis,—what.</small>

Hypotheses have thus no other end than to satisfy the desire of the mind to reduce the objects of its knowledge to unity and system; and they do this in recalling them, *ad interim*, to some principle, through which the mind is enabled to comprehend them. From this view of their

<small>Explication. Hypothesis,—its end.</small>

INDUCTION AND ANALOGY. 155

nature, it is manifest how far they are permissible, and how far they are even useful and expedient; throwing altogether out of account the possibility, that what is at first assumed as hypothetical, may, subsequently, be proved true.

When our experience has revealed to us a certain correspondence among a number of objects, we are determined, by an original principle of our nature, to suppose the existence of a more extensive correspondence than our observation has already proved, or may ever be able to establish. This tendency to generalize our knowledge by the judgment,—that where much has been found accordant, all will be found accordant,—is not properly a conclusion deduced from premises, but an original principle, of our nature, which we may call that of *Logical*, or perhaps better, that of *Philosophical, Presumption*. This Presumption is of two kinds; it is either Induction or Analogy, which, though usually confounded, are, however, to be carefully distinguished. I shall commence the consideration of these by the following paragraph.

¶ XVIII. If we have uniformly observed that a number of objects of the same class (genus or species) possess in common a certain attribute, we are disposed to conclude that this attribute is possessed by all the objects of that class. This conclusion is properly called an *Inference of Induction*. Again, if we have observed that two or more things agree in several internal and essential characters, we are disposed to conclude that they agree, likewise, in all other essential characters, that is, that they are constituents of the same class (genus or species). This conclusion is properly called an *Inference of Analogy*.

Par. XVIII. Induction and Analogy.

The principle by which, in either case, we are disposed to extend our inferences beyond the limits of experience, is a natural or ultimate principle of intelligence; and may be called the principle of *Logical*, or, more properly, of *Philosophical Presumption.*

Explication. Induction and Analogy, — their agreement and difference.

The reasoning by Induction and the reasoning by Analogy have this in common, that they both conclude from something observed to something not observed; from something within to something beyond the sphere of actual experience. They differ, however, in this, that, in Induction, that which is observed and from which the inference is drawn to that which is not observed, is a unity in plurality; whereas, in Analogy, it is a plurality in unity. In other words, in Induction, we look to the one in the many; in Analogy we look to the many in the one; and while in both we conclude to the unity in totality, we do this, in Induction, from the recognized unity in plurality, in Analogy, from the recognized plurality in unity. Thus, as induction rests upon the principle, that what belongs (or does not belong) to many things of the same kind, belongs, (or does not belong) to all things of the same kind; so analogy rests upon the principle,—that things which have many observed attributes in common, have other not observed attributes in common likewise. It is hardly necessary to remark that we are now speaking of Induction and Analogy, not as principles of Pure Logic, and as necessitated by the fundamental laws of thought, but of these as means of acquiring knowledge, and as legitimated by the conditions of objective reality. In Pure Logic, Analogy has no place, and only that Induction is admitted, in which all the several parts are supposed to legitimate the inference to the whole. Applied Induction, on the contrary, rests on the constancy,—the uniformity of nature, and on the instinctive expectation we have of this stability. This constitutes what has been called the principle of *Logical Presumption*, though perhaps it might, with greater propriety, be called the principle of *Philosophical Presumption*. We shall now consider these severally; and, first, of Induction.

An Induction is the enumeration of the parts, in order to legitimate a judgment in regard to the whole. Now, the parts may either be individuals or particulars, strictly so called. I say strictly so called, for you are aware that the term *particular* is very commonly employed, not only to denote the species, as contained under a genus, but, likewise, to denote the individual, as contained under a species. Using, however, the two terms in their proper significations, I say, if the parts are individual or singular things, the induction is then called *Individual;* whereas if the parts be species or subaltern genera, the induction then obtains the name of *Special*. An example of the Individual Induction is given, were we to argue thus,—*Mercury, Venus, the Earth, Mars, etc., are bodies in themselves opaque, and which borrow their light from the sun. But Mercury, Venus, etc., are planets. Therefore, all planets are opaque, and borrow their light from the sun.* An example of the special is given, were we to argue as follows,—*Quadrupeds, birds, fishes, the amphibia, etc., all have a nervous system. But quadrupeds, birds, etc., are animals. Therefore all animals* (though it is not yet detected in some) *have a nervous system.* Now, here it is manifest that Special rests upon Individual Induction,

Induction,—what.

Of two kinds,—Individual and Special.

and that, in the last result, all induction is individual. For we can assert nothing concerning species, unless what we assert of them has been previously observed in their constituent singulars.

For a legitimate Induction there are requisite at least two conditions. In the first place, it is necessary, That the partial (and this word I use as including both the terms *individual* and *particular,)*—I say, it is necessary that the partial judgments out of which the total or general judgment is inferred, be all of the same quality. For if one even of the partial judgments had an opposite quality, the whole induction would be subverted. Hence it is that we refute universal judgments founded on an imperfect induction, by bringing what is called an instance *(instantia)*, that is, by adducing a thing belonging to the same class or notion, in reference to which the opposite holds true. For example, the general assertion, *All dogs bark*, is refuted by the instance of the dogs of Labrador or California (I forget which),—these do not bark. In like manner, the general assertion, *No quadruped is oviparous*, is refuted by the instance of the *Ornithorhynchus Paradoxus*. But that the universal judgment must have the same quality as the partial, is self-evident; for this judgment is simply the assertion of something to be true of all which is true of many.

<small>The two conditions of legitimate Induction,—First.</small>

The second condition required is, That a competent number of the partial objects from which the induction departs, should have been observed, for otherwise the comprehension of other objects under the total judgment would be rash. What is the number of such objects, which amounts to a

<small>Second.</small>

competent induction, it is not possible to say in general. In some cases, the observation of a very few particular or individual examples is sufficient to warrant an assertion in regard to the whole class ; in others, the total judgment is hardly competent, until our observation has gone through each of its constituent parts. This distinction is founded on the difference of essential and unessential characters. If the character be essential to the several objects, a comparatively limited observation is necessary to legitimate our general conclusion. For example, it would require a far less induction to prove that all animals breathe, than to prove that the mamalia, and the mamalia alone, have lateral lobes to the cerebellum. For the one is seen to be a function necessary to animal life; the other, as far as our present knowledge reaches, appears only as an arbitrary concomitant. The difference of essential and accidental is, however, one itself founded on induction, and varies according to the greater or less perfection to which this has been carried. In the progress of science, the lateral lobes of the cerebellum may appear to future physiologists as necessary a condition of the function of suckling their young, as the organs of breathing appear to us of circulation and of life.

To sum up the Doctrine of Induction,—"This is more certain, 1°, In proportion to the number and diversity of the objects observed ;— 2°, In proportion to the accuracy with which the observation and comparison have been conducted ; —3°, In proportion as the agreement of the objects is clear and precise ; — and, 4°, In proportion as it has been thoroughly explored, whether there exist exceptions or not."

Summary of the doctrine of Induction

Almost all induction is, however, necessarily imperfect ; and Logic can inculcate nothing more important on the investigators of nature than that sobriety of mind, which regards all its past observations only as hypothetically true, only as relatively complete, and which, consequently, holds the mind open to every new observation, which may correct and limit its former judgments.

So much for Induction ; now for Analogy. Analogy, in general, means proportion, or a similarity of relations. Thus, to judge analogically, or according to analogy, is to judge things by the similarity of their relations. Thus, when we judge that as two is to four, so is eight to sixteen, we judge that they are analogically identical ; that is, though the sums in other respects are different, they agree in this, that as two is the half of four, so eight is the half of sixteen.

Analogy,—what.

In common language, however, this propriety of the term is not preserved. For *by analogy* is not always meant merely *by proportion*, but frequently *by comparison—by relation*, or simply *by similarity*. In so far as Analogy constitutes a particular kind of reasoning from the individual or particular to the universal, it signifies an inference from the partial similarity of two or more things to their complete or total similarity. For example, — *This disease corresponds in many symptoms with those we have observed in typhus fevers; it will, therefore, correspond in all, that is, it is a typhus fever.*

Like Induction, Analogy has two essential requisites. In the first place, it is necessary that of two or more things a certain number of attributes should have observed, in order to ground the inference that they also agree in those other attributes, which it has not yet been ascertained that they possess. It is evident that in proportion to the number of

Has two essential conditions,—First.

points observed, in which the things compared together coincide, in the same proportion can it be with safety assumed, that there exists a common principle in these things, on which depends the similarity in the points known as in the points unknown.

In the second place, it is required that the predicates already observed should neither be all negative nor all contingent; but that some at least should be positive and necessary. Mere negative characters denote only what the thing is not; and contingent characters need not be present in the thing at all. In regard to negative attributes, the inference, that two things, to which a number of qualities do not belong, and which are, consequently, similar to each other only in a negative point of view,—that these things are, therefore, absolutely and positively similar, is highly improbable. But that the judgment in reference to the compared things (say A and X) must be of the same quality (*i. e.* either both affirmative or both negative), is self-evident. For if it be said A *is* B, X *is not* B, A *is not* C, X *is* C; their harmony or similarity is subverted, and we should rather be warranted in arguing their discord and dissimilarity in other points. And here it is to be noticed that Analogy differs from Induction in this, that it is not limited to one quality, but that it admits of a mixture of both.

In regard to contingent attributes, it is equally manifest that the analogy cannot proceed exclusively upon them. For, if two things coincide in certain accidental attributes (for example, two men in respect of stature, age, and dress,) the supposition that there is a common principle, and a general similarity founded thereon, is very unlikely.

To conclude : Analogy is certain in proportion, 1°, To the number of congruent observations ; 2°, To the number of congruent characters observed ; 3°, To the importance of these characters and their essentiality to the objects ; and, 4°, To the certainty that the characters really belong to the objects, and that a partial correspondence exists. Like Induction, Analogy can only pretend at best to a high degree of probability ; it may have a high degree of certainty, but it never reaches to necessity.

Summary of the doctrine of Analogy.

Comparing these two processes together : The Analogical is distinguished from the Inductive in this —that Induction regards a single predicate in many subjects as the attribute Z in A, in B, in C, in D, in E, in F, etc. ; and as these many belong to one class, say Q ; it is inferred that Z will, likewise, be met with in the other things belonging to this class, that is, in all Qs. On the other hand, Analogy regards many attributes in one subject (say m, n, o, p, in A) ; and as these many are in part found in another subject (say m, and n, in B), it is concluded that, in that second thing, there will also be found the other attributes (say o and p). Through Induction we, therefore, endeavor to prove that one character belongs (or does not belong) to all the things of a certain class, because it belongs (or does not belong) to many things of that class. Through Analogy on the other hand, we seek to prove that all the characters of a thing belong (or do not belong) to another or several others, because many of these characters belong to this other or these others. In the one it is proclaimed,— *One in many, therefore one in all.*—In the other it is proclaimed,—*Many in one, therefore all in one.*

Induction and Analogy compared together.

By these Processes of Induction and Analogy, as observed, we are unable to attain absolute certainty ;—a great probability is all that we can reach, and this for the simple reason, that it is impossible, under any condition, to infer the unobserved from the observed,— the whole from any proportion of the parts,—in the way of any rational necessity. Even from the requisites of Induction and Analogy, it is manifest that they bear the stamp of uncertainty ; inasmuch as they are unable to determine how many objects or how many characters must be observed, in order to draw the conclusion that the case is the same with all the other objects, or with all the other characters. It is possible only in one way to raise Induction and Analogy from mere probability to complete certainty,—viz., to demonstrate that the principles which lie at the root of these processes, and which we have already stated, are either necessary laws of thought, or necessary laws of nature. To demonstrate that they are necessary laws of thought is impossible ; for Logic not only does not allow inference from many to all, but expressly rejects it. Again, to demonstrate that they are necessary laws of nature is equally impossible. This has indeed been attempted, from the uniformity of nature, but in vain. For it is incompetent to evince the necessity of the inference of Induction and Analogy from the fact denominated *the law of nature ;* seeing that this law itself can only be discovered by the way of Induction and Analogy. In this attempted demonstration there is thus the most glaring *petitio principii.* The result which has been previously given remains, therefore, intact :—Induction and Analogy guarantee no perfect certainty, but only a high degree of probability, while all probability rests at best upon Induction and Analogy, and nothing else.

Marginal note: Induction and Analogy do not afford absolute certainty.

LECTURE VII.—MODIFIED METHODOLOGY.

SECTION I.—OF THE ACQUISITION OF KNOWLEDGE.

I. EXPERIENCE—B. FOREIGN :—ORAL TESTIMONY— ITS CREDIBILITY.

HAVING, in our last Lecture, terminated the Doctrine of Empirical Knowledge, considered as obtained Immediately,—that is, through the exercise of our own powers of Observation,—we are now to enter on the doctrine of Empirical Knowledge considered as obtained Mediately,—that is, through the Experience of Other Men. The following paragraph will afford you a general notion of the nature and kinds of this knowledge.

Foreign Experience.

¶ XIX. A matter of Observation or Empirical Knowledge can only be obtained Mediately, that is, by one individual from another, through an enouncement declaring it to be true. This enouncement is called, in the most extensive sense of the word, a *Witnessing* or *Testimony (testimonium);* and the person by whom it is made is, in the same sense, called a *Witness*, or *Testifier (testis)*. The object of the testimony is called the *Fact (factum);* and its validity constitutes what is styled *Historical Credibility (credibilitas historica)*. To estimate this credibility, it is requisite to consider—

Par. XIX. Testimony.

1°, The Subjective Trustworthiness of the Witnesses (*fides testium*), and 2°, The Objective Probability of the Fact itself. The former is founded partly on the Sincerity, and partly on the Competence, of the Witness. The latter depends on the Absolute and Relative Possibility of the Fact itself. Testimony is either Immediate or Mediate. Immediate, where the fact reported is the object of a Personal Experience; Mediate, where the fact reported is the object of a Foreign Experience.

It is manifest that Foreign Experience, or the experience of other men, is astricted to the same laws, and its certainty measured by the same criteria, as the experience we carry through ourselves. But the experience of the individual is limited, when compared with the experience of the species; and if men did not possess the means of communicating to each other the results of their several observations,—were they unable to coöperate in accumulating a stock of knowledge, and in carrying on the progress of discovery,—they would never have risen above the very lowest steps in the acquisition of science. But to this mutual communication they are competent; and each individual is thus able to appropriate to his own benefit the experience of his fellow-men, and to confer on them in return the advantages which his own observations may supply. But it is evident that this reciprocal communication of their respective experiences among men, can only be effected inasmuch as one is able to inform another of what he has himself observed, and that the vehicle of this information can only be some enouncement in conventional signs of one character or another. -The enouncement of what has been observed is, as stated in the paragraph, called

Explication.

a witnessing,—a bearing witness,—a testimony, etc., these terms being employed in their wider acceptation; and he by whom this declaration is made, and on whose veracity it rests, is called a *witness, voucher*, or *testifier (testis)*. The term *testimony*, I may notice, is sometimes, by an abusive metonym, employed for *witness;* and the word *evidence* is often ambiguously used for *testimony*, and for the bearer of testimony,—*the witness*.

Such an enouncement,—such a testimony, is, however, necessary for others, only when the experience which it communicates is beyond the compass of their own observation. Hence it follows, that matters of reasoning are not proper objects of testimony, since matters of reasoning, as such, neither can rest, nor ought to rest, on the observations of others; for a proof of their certainty is equally competent to all, and may by all be obtained in the manner in which it was originally obtained by those who may bear witness to their truth. And hence it further follows, that matters of experience alone are proper objects of testimony; and of matters of experience themselves, such only as are beyond the sphere of our personal experience. Testimony, in the strictest sense of the term, therefore, is the communication of an experience, or, what amounts to the same thing, the report of an observed phænomenon, made to those whose own experience or observation has not reached so far.

The proper object of Testimony.

The object of testimony, as stated in the paragraph, is called the *fact;* the validity of a testimony is called *historical credibility*. The testimony is either immediate or mediate. Immediate when the witness has himself observed the fact to which he testifies; mediate, when the

The Fact. Historical credibility.

witness has not himself had experience of this fact, but has received it on the testimony of others. The former, the immediate witness, is commonly styled an *eye-witness (testis oculatus)*; and the latter, the mediate witness, an *ear-witness (testis auritas)*. The superiority of immediate to mediate testimony is expressed by Plautus, "*Pluris est oculatus testis unus, quam auriti decem.*" These denominations, *eye* and *ear witness*, are however, as synonyms of *immediate* and *mediate witness*, not always either applicable or correct. The person on whose testimony a fact is mediately reported, is called the *guarantee*, or he on whose authority it rests; and the guarantee himself may be again either an immediate or a mediate witness. In the latter case he is called a *second-hand* or *intermediate witness;* and his testimony is commonly styled *hearsay evidence*. Further, Testimony, whether immediate or mediate, is either *partial* or *complete;* either *consistent* or *contradictory*. These distinctions require no comment. Finally, testimony is either *direct* or *indirect;* direct, when the witness has no motive but that of making known the fact; indirect, when he is actuated to this by other ends.

The only question in reference to Testimony is that which regards its Credibility; and the question concerning the credibility of the witness may be comprehended under that touching the Credibility of Testimony. The order I shall follow in the subsequent observations is this,—I shall, in the first place, consider the Credibility of Testimony in general; and, in the second, consider the Credibility of Testimony in its particular forms of Immediate and Mediate.

First, then, in regard to the Credibility of Testimony in general;—When we inquire whether a certain testimony is, or is not, deserving of credit, there are two things to be considered: 1°, The Object of the Testimony, that is, the fact or facts for the truth of which the Testimony vouches; and, 2°, The Subject of the Testimony, that is, the person or persons by whom the testimony is borne. The question, therefore, concerning the Credibility of testimony, thus naturally subdivides itself into two. Of these questions, the first asks, What are the conditions of the credibility of a testimony by reference to what is testified, that is, in relation to the Object of the testimony? The second asks,— What are the conditions of the credibility of a testimony by him who testifies, that is, in relation to the Subject of the testimony? Of these in their order.

On the first question.—" In regard to the matter testified, that is, in regard to the object of the testimony; it is, first of all, a requisite condition, that what is reported to be true should be possible, both absolutely, or as an object of the Elaborative Faculty, and relatively, or as an object of the Presentative Faculties,—Perception, External or Internal. A thing is possible absolutely, or in itself, when it can be construed to thought, that is, when it is not inconsistent with the logical laws of thinking; a thing is relatively possible as an object of Perception, External or Internal, when it can affect Sense or Self-consciousness, and, through such affection, determine its apprehension by one or other of these faculties. A testimony is, therefore, to be unconditionally rejected, if

Marginal notes: I. Credibility of Testimony in general. 1°, The Object of the Testimony. Its absolute Possibility.

the fact which it reports be either in itself impossible, or impossible as an object of the Presentative Faculties. But the impossibility of a thing, as an object of these faculties, must be decided either upon physical, or upon metaphysical, principles. A thing is physically impossible as an object of sense, when the existence itself, or its perception by us, is, by the laws of the material world, impossible. It is metaphysically impossible, when the object itself, or its perception, is possible neither through a natural nor through a supernatural, agency. But, to establish the metaphysical impossibility of a thing, it is not sufficient that its existence cannot be explained by the ordinary laws of nature, or even that its existence should appear repugnant with these laws; it is requisite that an universal and immutable law of nature should have been demonstrated to exist, and that this law would be subverted if the fact in question were admitted to be physically possible. In like manner, to constitute the metaphysical impossibility of a thing, it is by no means enough to show that it is not explicable on natural laws, or even that any natural law stands opposed to it; it is further requisite to prove that the intervention even of supernatural agency is incompetent to its production, that its existence would involve the violation of some necessary principle of reason.

Physical and Metaphysical Impossibility.

To establish the credibility of a testimony, in so far as this is regulated by the nature of its object, there is, besides the proof of the absolute possibility of this object, required also a proof of its relative possibility; that is, there must not only be no contradiction between its necessary attributes,— the attributes by which it must be thought,—but no contra-

Relative Possibility of an object.

diction between the attributes actually assigned to it by the testimony. A testimony, therefore, which, *qua* testimony, is self-contradictory, can lay no claim to credibility; for what is self-contradictory is logically suicidal. And here the only question is,—Does the testimony, *qua* testimony, contradict itself? for if the repugnancy arise from an opinion of the witness, apart from which the testimony as such would still stand undisproved, in that case the testimony is not at once to be repudiated as false. For example, it would be wrong to reject a testimony to the existence of a thing, because the witness had to his evidence of its observed reality annexed some conjecture in regard to its origin or cause. For the latter might well be shown to be absurd, and yet the former would remain unshaken. It is, therefore, always to be observed,—that it is only the self-contradiction of a testimony, *qua* testimony, that is, the self-contradiction of the fact itself, which is peremptorily and irrevocably subversive of its credibility.

We now proceed to the second question; that is, to consider in general the Credibility of a Testimony by reference to its subject, that is, in relation to the Personal Trustworthiness of the Witness. The trustworthiness of a witness consists of two elements or conditions. In the first place, he must be willing, in the second place, he must be able, to report the truth. The first of these elements is the Honesty,—the Sincerity,—the Veracity; the second is the Competency of the Witness. Both are equally necessary, and if one or other be deficient, the testimony becomes altogether null. These constituents, likewise, do not infer each other; for it frequently happens that where the honesty

2°, The Subject of the Testimony, or personal trustworthiness of the Witness. This consists of two elements:—(a) Honesty or Veracity.

is greatest the competency is least, and where the competency is greatest, the honesty is least. But when the veracity of a witness is established, there is established also a presumption of his competency; for an honest man will not bear evidence to a point in regard to which his recollection is not precise, or to the observation of which he had not accorded the requisite attention. In truth, when a fact depends on the testimony of a single witness, the competency of that witness is solely guaranteed by his honesty. In regard to the honesty of a witness,—this, though often admitting of the highest probability, never admits of absolute certainty; for, though in many cases, we may know enough of the general character of the witness to rely with perfect confidence on his veracity, in no case can we look into the heart, and observe the influence which motives have actually had upon his volitions. We are, however, compelled, in many of the most important concerns of our existence, to depend on the testimony, and, consequently, to confide in the sincerity, of others. But from the moral constitution of human nature, we are warranted in presuming on the honesty of a witness; and this presumption is enhanced in proportion as the following circumstances concur in its confirmation. In the first place, a witness is to be presumed veracious in this case, in proportion as his love of truth is already established from others. In the second place, a witness is to be presumed veracious, in proportion as he has fewer and weaker motives to falsify his testimony. In the third place, a witness is to be presumed veracious, in proportion to the likelihood of contradiction which his testimony would encounter, if he

The presumption of the Honesty of a Witness enhanced by certain circumstances.

deviated from the truth. So much for the Sincerity, Honesty, or Veracity of a witness.

In regard to the Competency or Ability of a witness,—this, in general, depends on the supposition that he has had it in his power correctly to observe the fact to which he testifies, and correctly to report it. The presumption in favor of the competence of a witness rises in proportion as the following conditions are fulfilled:—In the first place, he must be presumed competent in reference to the case in hand, in proportion as his general ability to observe and to communicate his observation has been established in other cases. In the second place, the competency of a witness must be presumed, in proportion as in the particular case a lower and commoner amount of ability is requisite rightly to observe, and rightly to report the observation. In the third place, the competency of a witness is to be presumed, in proportion as it is not to be presumed that his observation was made or communicated at a time when he was unable correctly to make or correctly to communicate it. So much for the Competency of a witness.

(b) Competency of a Witness.

Circumstances by which the presumption of competency is enhanced.

Now, when both the good will and the ability, that is, when both the Veracity and Competence of a witness have been sufficiently established, the credibility of his testimony is not to be invalidated because the fact which it goes to prove is one out of the ordinary course of experience. Thus it would be false to assert, with Hume, that miracles, that is, suspensions of the ordinary laws of nature, are incapable of proof, because contradicted by what we have been able to observe. On the

The credibility of Testimony not invalidated because the fact testified is one out of the ordinary course of experience.

contrary, where the trustworthiness of a witness or witnesses is unimpeachable, the very circumstance that the object is one in itself unusual and marvellous, adds greater weight to the testimony ; for this very circumstance would itself induce men of veracity and intelligence to accord a more attentive scrutiny to the fact, and secure from them a more accurate report of their observation.

The result of what has now been stated in regard to the credibility of Testimony in general, is :—

Summary regarding the Credibility of Testimony in general. That a testimony is entitled to credit when the requisite conditions, both on the part of the object and on the part of the subject, have been fulfilled. On the part of the object these are fulfilled when the object is absolutely possible, as an object of the higher faculty of experience,—the Understanding,—the Elaborative Faculty, and relatively possible, as an object of the lower or subsidiary faculties of experience,— Sense, and Self-consciousness. In this case, the testimony, *qua* testimony, does not contradict itself. On the part of the subject the requisite conditions are fulfilled when the trustworthiness, that is, the veracity and competency of the witness, is beyond reasonable doubt. In regard to the veracity of the witness,—this cannot be reasonably doubted, when there is no positive ground on which to discredit the sincerity of the witness, and when the only ground of doubt lies in the mere general possibility of deception. And in reference to the competency of a witness,—this is exposed to no reasonable objection, when the ability of the witness to observe and to communicate the fact in testimony cannot be disallowed. Having, therefore, concluded the consideration of testimony in general, we proceed to treat of it in special, that is, in so far as it is viewed either as Immediate or as Mediate. Of these in their order.

The special consideration of Testimony, when that testimony is Immediate.—An immediate testimony, or testimony at first hand, is one in which the fact reported is an object of the proper or personal experience of the reporter. Now it is manifest, that an immediate witness is in general better entitled to credit than a witness at second hand; and his testimony rises in probability, in proportion as the requisites, already specified, both on the part of its object and on the part of its subject, are fulfilled. An immediate testimony is, therefore, entitled to credit,—1°, In proportion to the greater ability with which the observation has been made; 2°, In proportion to the less impediment in the way of the observation being perfectly accomplished; 3°, In proportion as what was observed could be fully and accurately remembered; and, 4°, In proportion as the facts observed and remembered have been communicated by intelligible and unambiguous signs.

II. Testimony in special, as Immediate and Mediate.

1°, Immediate Testimony.

Conditions of its Credibility.

Now, whether all these conditions of a higher credibility be fulfilled in the case of any immediate testimony,—this cannot be directly and at once ascertained; it can only be inferred, with greater or less certainty, from the qualities of the witness; and, consequently, the validity of a testimony can only be accurately estimated from a critical knowledge of the personal character of the witness, as given in his intellectual and moral qualities, and in the circumstances of his life, which have concurred to modify and determine these. The veracity of a witness either is, or is not, exempt from doubt; and, in the latter case, it may not only lie open to doubt,

Whether all these conditions are fulfilled in the case of any immediate testimony, cannot be directly ascertained.

but even be exposed to suspicion. If the sincerity of the witness be indubitable, a direct testimony is always preferable to an indirect; for a direct testimony being made with the sole intent of establishing the certainty of the fact in question, the competency of the witness is less exposed to objection. If, on the contrary, the sincerity of the witness be not beyond a doubt, and, still more, if it be actually suspected, in that case an indirect testimony is of higher cogency than a direct; for the indirect testimony being given with another view than merely to establish the fact in question, the intention of the witness to falsify the truth of the fact has not so strong a presumption in its favor. If both the sincerity and the competency of the witness are altogether indubitable, it is then of no importance whether the truth of the fact be vouched for by a single witness, or by a plurality of witnesses. On the other hand, if the sincerity and competency of the witness be at all doubtful, the credibility of a testimony will be greater, the greater the number of the witnesses by whom the fact is corroborated. But here it is to be considered, that when there are a plurality of testimonies to the same fact, these testimonies are either consistent or inconsistent. If the testimonies be consistent, and the sincerity and competency of all the witnesses complete, in that case the testimony attains the highest degree of probability of which any testimony is capable. Again, if the witnesses be inconsistent,—on this hypothesis two cases are possible; for either their discrepancy is negative, or it is positive. A negative discrepancy arises, where one witness passes over in silence what another witness positively avers. A positive discrepancy arises, where one witness

When testimony attains the highest degree of probability.

Negative and Positive Discrepancy.

explicitly affirms something, which something another witness explicitly denies. When the difference of testimonies is merely negative, we may suppose various causes of the silence; and, therefore, the positive averment of one witness to a fact is not disproved by the mere circumstance that the same fact is omitted by another. But if it be made out, that the witness who omits mention of the fact could not have been ignorant of that fact had it taken place, and, at the same time, that he could not have passed it over without violating every probability of human action,—in this case, the silence of the one witness manifestly derogates from the credibility of the other witness, and in certain circumstances may annihilate it altogether. Where, again, the difference is positive, the discrepancy is of greater importance, because (though there are certainly exceptions to the rule) an overt contradiction is, in general and in itself, of stronger cogency than a mere non-confirmation by simple silence. Now the positive discrepancy of testimonies either admits of conciliation, or it does not. In the former case, the credibility of the several testimonies stands intact; and the discrepancy among the witnesses is to be accounted for by such circumstances as explain, without invalidating, the testimony considered in itself. In the latter case, one testimony manifestly detracts from the credibility of another; for of incompatible testimonies, while both cannot be true, the one must be false, when reciprocally contradictory, or they may both be false, when reciprocally contrary. In this case, the whole question resolves itself into one of the greater or less trustworthiness of the opposing witnesses. Is the trustworthiness of the counter-witnesses equally great? In that case, neither of the conflictive testimonies is to be admitted. Again, is the trustworthiness of the witnesses not upon a par ? In that case, the testimony of the witness whose trustworthiness is the greater, obtains the preference,—and this more especially if the credibility of the other witnesses is suspected.

So much for the Credibility of Testimony, considered in Special, in so far as that testimony is Immediate or at First Hand; and I now, in the second place, pass on to consider likewise in special, the Credibility of Testimony, in so far as that testimony is Mediate, or at Second Hand.

A Mediate Testimony is one where the fact is an object not of Personal, but of Foreign Experi-
2°, Mediate Testimony. ence. Touching the credibility of a mediate testimony, this supposes that the report of the immediate, and that the report of the mediate, witness are both trustworthy,—this we are either of ourselves able to determine, viz., from our personal acquaintance with its veracity and competence; or we are unable of ourselves to do this, in which case the credibility of the immediate must be taken upon the authority of the mediate witness. Here, however, it is necessary for us to be aware, that the mediate witness is possessed of the ability requisite to estimate the credibility of the immediate witness, and of the honesty to communicate the truth without retrenchment or falsification. But if the trustworthiness both of the mediate and of the immediate witness be sufficiently established, it is of no consequence, in regard to the credibility of a testimony, whether it be at first hand or at second. Nay, the testimony of a mediate may even tend to confirm the testimony of an immediate witness, when his own competence fairly to appreciate the report of the immediate witness is indubitable. If, however, the credibility of the immediate witness be unimpeachable, but

not so the credibility of the mediate, in that case the mediate testimony, in respect of its authority, is inferior to the immediate, and this in the same proportion as the credibility of the second hand witness is inferior to that of the witness at first hand. Further, mediate witnesses are either Proximate or Remote; and, in both cases, either Independent or Dependent. The trustworthiness of proximate witnesses is, in general, greater than the trustworthiness of remote; and the credibility of independent witnesses greater than the credibility of dependent. The remote witness is unworthy of belief, when the intermediate links are wanting between him and the original witness; and the dependent witness deserves no credit, when that on which his evidence depends is recognized as false or unestablished. Mediate testimonies are, likewise, either direct or indirect; and, likewise, when more than one, either reciprocally congruent or conflictive. In both cases the credibility of the witnesses is to be determined in the same manner as if the testimonies were immediate.

<small>Mediate Witnesses are either Proximate or Remote, and either Independent or Dependent.</small>

The testimony of a plurality of mediate witnesses, where there is no recognized immediate witness, is called a *rumor*, if the witnesses be contemporaneous; and a *tradition* if the witnesses be chronologically successive. These are both less entitled to credit, in proportion as in either case a fiction or falsification of the fact is comparatively easy, and, consequently, comparatively probable.

<small>Rumor,—what. Tradition.</small>

LECTURE VIII.—MODIFIED METHODOLOGY.

SECTION I.—OF THE ACQUISITION OF KNOWLEDGE.

I. EXPERIENCE. — B. FOREIGN : — RECORDED TESTIMONY AND WRITINGS IN GENERAL.

II. SPECULATION.

Criticism of Recorded Testimony and of Writings in general.

IN our last Lecture, we were engaged in the consideration of Testimony, and the Principles by which its Credibility is governed,—on the supposition always that we possess the veritable report of the witness whose testimony it professes to be, and on the supposition that we are at no loss to understand its meaning and purport. But questions may arise in regard to these points, and, therefore, there is a further critical process requisite, in order to establish the Authenticity,—the Integrity, and the Signification, of the documents in which the testimony is conveyed. This leads to the important subject,—the Criticism of Recorded Testimony, and of Writings in general. I shall comprise the heads of the following observations on this subject in the ensuing paragraph.

¶ XX. The examination and judgment of Writings professing to contain the testimony of certain witnesses, and of Writings in General professing to be the work of certain authors, is of two parts. For the inquiry regards either, 1°, The Authenticity of the document, that is, whether it be, in whole or in part, the product of its ostensible author; for ancient writings in particular are frequently suppositious or interpolated; or, 2°, It regards the Meaning of the words of which it is composed, for these, especially when in languages now dead, are frequently obscure. The former of these problems is resolved by the *Art of Criticism (Critica,)* in the stricter sense of the term; the latter by the *Art of Interpretation (Exegetica* or *Hermeneutica.)* Criticism is of two kinds. If it be occupied with the criteria of the authenticity of a writing in its totality, or in its principal parts, it is called the *Higher*, and sometimes the *Internal, Criticism*. If, again, it consider only the integrity of particular words and phrases, it is called the *Lower*, and sometimes the *External, Criticism*. The former of these may perhaps be best styled the *Criticism of Authenticity*;—the latter, the *Criticism of Integrity*.

Par. XX. Criticism and Interpretation.

The problem which Interpretation has to solve is,— To discover and expound the meaning of a writer, from the words in which his thoughts are expressed. It departs from the principle, that however manifold be the possible meanings of the expressions, the sense of the writer is one. Interpretation, by reference to its sources or subsidia, has been divided into the *Grammatical*, the *Historical*, and the *Philosophical*, *Exegesis*.

Testimonies, especially when the ostensible witnesses themselves can no longer be interrogated, may be subjected to an examination under various forms; and this examination is in fact indispensable, seeing not only that a false testimony may be substituted for a true, and a testimony true upon the whole may yet be falsified in its parts,—a practice which prevailed to a great extent in ancient times; while at the same time the meaning of the testimony, by reason either of the foreign character of the language in which it is expressed, or of the foreign character of thought in which it is conceived, may be obscure and undetermined. The examination of a testimony is twofold, inasmuch as it is either an examination of its Authenticity and Integrity, or an examination of its Meaning. This twofold process of examination is applicable to testimonies of every kind, but it becomes indispensable when the testimony has been recorded in writing, and when this, from its antiquity, has come down to us only in transcripts, indefinitely removed from the original, and when the witnesses are men differing greatly from ourselves in language, manners, customs, and associations of thought. The solution of the problem,—By what laws are the authenticity or spuriousness, the integrity or corruption, of a writing to be determined, —constitutes the Art of Criticism, in its stricter signification *(Critica)*; and the solution of the problem,—By what law is the sense or meaning of a writing to be determined, —constitutes the Art of Interpretation or Exposition *(Hermeneutica, Exegetica)*. In theory, Criticism ought to precede Interpretation, for

Explication.

The examination of a testimony twofold,
—of its Authenticity and Integrity, and of its Meaning.

Criticism.

Interpretation.

the question,—Who has spoken, naturally arises before the question,—How what has been spoken is to be understood. But in practice, criticism and interpretation cannot be separated; for in application they proceed hand in hand.

First, then, of Criticism; and the question that presents itself in the threshold is,—What are its Definition and Divisions? Under Criticism is to be understood the complement of logical rules, by which the authenticity or spuriousness, the integrity or interpolation, of a writing is to be judged. The problems which it proposes to answer are,—1°, Does a writing really proceed from the author to whom it is ascribed; and 2°, Is a writing, as we possess it, in all its parts the same as it came from the hands of its author. The system of fundamental rules, which are supposed in judging of the authenticity and integrity of every writing, constitutes what is called the *Doctrine of Universal Criticism;* and the system of particular rules, by which the authenticity and integrity of writings of a certain kind are judged, constitutes the doctrine of what is called *Special Criticism.* It is manifest, from the nature of Logic, that the doctrine of Universal Criticism is alone within its sphere. Now Universal Criticism is conversant either with the authenticity or spuriousness of a writing considered as a whole, or with the integrity or interpolation of certain parts. In the former case it is called *Higher,* in the latter, *Lower, Criticism;* but these denominations are inappropriate. The one criticism has also been styled the *Internal,* the other the *External;* but these appellations are, likewise, excep-

marginalia: I. Criticism. Its problems. Universal Criticism. Special Criticism. Universal Criticism alone within the sphere of Logic. Its Divisions.

tionable; and, perhaps, it would be preferable to call the former the *Criticism of the Authenticity*, the latter, the *Criticism of the Integrity*, of a work. I shall consider these in particular; and, first, of the Criticism of Authenticity.

A proof of the authenticity of a writing, more especially of an ancient writing, can be rested only upon two grounds, —an Internal and an External,—and on these either apart or in combination. By *internal grounds*, we mean those indications of authenticity which the writing itself affords. By *external grounds*, we denote the testimony borne by other works, of a corresponding antiquity, to the authenticity of the writing in question.

<small>1. Criticism of Authenticity.</small>

In regard to the Internal Grounds;—it is evident, without entering upon details, that these cannot of themselves, that is, apart from the external grounds, afford evidence capable of establishing beyond a doubt the authenticity of an ancient writing; for we can easily conceive that an able and learned forger may accommodate his fabrications both to all the general circumstances of time, place, people, and language, under which it is supposed to have been written, and even to all the particular circumstances of the style, habit of thought, personal relations, etc., of the author by whom it professes to have been written, so that everything may militate for, and nothing militate against, its authenticity.

<small>(a) Internal Grounds. These of themselves not sufficient to establish the authenticity of a writing.</small>

But if our criticism from the internal grounds alone be, on the one hand, impotent to establish, it is, on the other, omnipotent to disprove. For it is sufficient to show that a writing is in essential parts, that is, parts which cannot be separated

<small>But omnipotent to disprove this.</small>

from the whole, in opposition to the known manners, institutions, usages, etc., of that people with which it would, and must, have been in harmony, were it the product of the writer whose name it bears; that, on the contrary, it bears upon its face indications of another country or of a later age; and, finally, that it is at variance with the personal circumstances, the turn of mind, and the pitch of intellect, of its pretended author. And here it is to be noticed, that these grounds are only relatively internal; for we become aware of them originally only through the testimony of others, that is, through external grounds.

In regard to the External Grounds;—they, as I said, consist in the testimony, direct or indirect, given to the authenticity of the writing in question by other works of a competent antiquity. This testimony may be contained either in other and admitted writings of the supposed author himself; or in those of contemporary writers; or in those of writers approximating in antiquity. This testimony may also be given either directly by attribution of the disputed writing by title to the author; or indirectly, by quoting as his certain passages which are to be found in it. On this subject it is needless to go into detail, and it is hardly necessary to observe, that the proof of the authenticity is most complete when it proceeds upon the internal and external grounds together. I, therefore, pass on to the Criticism of Integrity.

(b)External Grounds.

When the authenticity of an ancient work has been established on external grounds, and been confirmed on internal, the integrity of this writing is not therewith proved; for it is very possible, and in ancient writings indeed very probable, that particular passages are either interpolated or corrupted.

2. Criticism of Integrity.

The authenticity of particular passages is to be judged of precisely by the same laws which regulate our criticism of the authenticity of the whole work. The proof most pertinent to the authenticity of particular passages is drawn—1°, From their acknowledgment by the author himself in other, and these unsuspected, works; 2°, From the attribution of them to the author by other writers of competent information; and, 3°, From the evidence of the most ancient MSS. On the other hand, a passage is to be obelized as spurious,—1°, When found to be repugnant to the general relations of time and place, and to the personal relations of the author; 2°, When wanting in the more ancient codices, and extant only in the more modern. A passage is suspicious, when any motive for its interpolation is manifest, even should we be unable to establish it as spurious. The differences which different copies of a writing exhibit in the particular passages, are called *various readings (variæ lectiones* or *lectiones variantes)*. Now, as of various readings only one can be the true, while they may all very easily be false, the problem which the criticism of Integrity proposes to solve is,—How is the genuine reading to be made out; and herein consists what is technically called the *Recension*, more properly the *Emendation*, of the text.

The Emendation of an ancient author may be of two kinds; the one of which may be called

Emendation of the text,—of two kinds, viz., Historical and Conjectural.

Historical, the other the *Conjectural*. The former of these founds upon historical data for its proof; the latter, again, proceeds on grounds which lie beyond the sphere of historical fact, and this for the very reason that historical fact is found incompetent to the restoration of the text to its original integrity. The historical emendation necessarily precedes the conjectural, because the object itself of emendation is wholly of an historical character, and because it is not permitted to attempt any other than an emendation on historical grounds, until, from these very grounds themselves, it be shown that the restitution of the text to its original integrity cannot be historically accomplished. Historical Emendation is again of two kinds, according as its judgment proceeds on external or on internal grounds. It founds upon external grounds, when the reasons for the truth or falsehood of a reading are derived from testimony; it founds upon internal grounds when the reasons for the truth or falsehood of a reading are derived from the writing itself. Historical emendation has thus a two-fold function to perform (and in its application to practice, these must always be performed in conjunction), viz., it has carefully to seek out and accurately to weigh both the external and internal reasons in support of the reading in dispute. Of external grounds the principal consists in the confirmation afforded by MSS., by printed editions which have immediately emanated from MSS., by ancient translations, and by passages quoted in ancient authors. The internal grounds are all derived either from the form, or from the contents, of the work itself. In reference to the form,—a reading is probable, in proportion as it corresponds to the general character of the language prevalent at the epoch when the work was written, and to the peculiar character of the language by which the author himself was distinguished. In reference to the contents,—a reading is probable, when it harmonizes with the context, that is, when it concurs with the other words of the particular passage in which it stands, in affording a meaning reasonable in itself,

Historical Emendation of two kinds,— External and Internal.

and conformable with the author's opinions, reasonings, and general character of thought.

It frequently happens, however, that, notwithstanding the uniformity of MSS., and other external subsidia, a reading cannot be recognized as genuine. In this case, it must be scientifically shown from the rules of criticism itself that this lection is corrupt. If the demonstration thus attempted be satisfactory, and if all external subsidia have been tried in vain, the critic is permitted to consider in what manner the corrupted passage can be restored to its integrity. And here the conjectural or divinatory emendation comes into play ; a process in which the power and efficiency of criticism and the genius of the critic are principally manifested.

Conjectural Emendation.

So much for Criticism, in its applications both to the Authenticity and to the Integrity of Writings. We have now to consider the general rules by which Interpretation, that is, the scientific process of expounding the Meaning of an author, is regulated.

By the *Art of Interpretation*, called likewise technically *Hermeneutic* or *Exegetic*, is meant the complement of logical laws, by which the sense of an ancient writing is to be evolved. Hermeneutic is either General or Special. General, when it contains those laws which apply to the interpretation of any writing whatever; Special, when it comprises those laws by which writings of a particular kind are to be expounded. The former of these alone is of logical concernment. The problem proposed for the Art of Interpretation to solve, is,—How are we to proceed in order to discover from the words of a writing that sole meaning which the author intended them to convey ? In

II. Interpretation.

General or Special.

the interpretation of a work, it is not, therefore, enough to show in what signification its words may be understood ; for it is required that we show in what signification they must. To the execution of this task two conditions are absolutely necessary ; 1°, That the interpreter should be thoroughly acquainted with the language itself in general, and with the language of the writer in particular ; and 2°, That the interpreter should be familiar with the subjects of which the writing treats. But these two requisites, though indispensable, are not of themselves sufficient. It is also of importance that the expositor should have a competent acquaintance with the author's personal circumstances and character of thought, and with the history and spirit of the age and country in which he lived. In regard to the interpretation itself,—it is to be again observed, that as a writer could employ expressions only in a single sense, so the result of the exposition ought to be not merely to show what meaning may possibly attach to the doubtful terms, but what meaning necessarily must. When, therefore, it appears that a passage is of doubtful import, the best preparative for a final determination of its meaning is, in the first place, to ascertain in how many different significations it may be construed, and then, by a process of exclusion, to arrive at the one veritable meaning. When, however, the obscurity cannot be removed, in that case it is the duty of the expositor, before abandoning his task, to evince that an interpretation of the passage is, without change, absolutely or relatively impossible.

As to the sources from whence the Interpretation is to be drawn,—these are three in all,— viz., 1°, The *Tractus literarum*, the words themselves, as they appear in MSS. ; 2°, The context, that is, the passage in immediate connection

<small>Sources of Interpretation.</small>

with the doubtful term ; 3°, Parallel or analogous passages in the same, or in other writings. How the interpretation drawn from these sources is to be applied, I shall not attempt to detail ; but pass on to a more generally useful and interesting subject.

So much for Experience or Observation, the first mean of scientific discovery, that, viz., by which we apprehend what is presented as contingent phænomena, and by whose process of Induction and Analogy we carry up individual into general facts. We have now to consider the other mean of scientific discovery, that, viz., by which, from the phænomena presented as contingent, we separate what is really necessary, and thus attain to the knowledge, not of merely generalized facts, but of universal laws. This mean may, for distinction's sake, be called *Speculation*, and its general nature I comprehend in the following paragraph.

Speculation the Second Means of Knowledge.

¶ XXI. When the mind does not rest contented with observing and classifying the objects of its experience, but, by a reflective analysis, sunders the concrete wholes presented to its cognition, throws out of account all that, as contingent, it can think away from, and concentrates its attention exclusively on those elements which, as necessary conditions of its own acts, it cannot but think ;—by this process it obtains the knowledge of a certain order of facts,—facts of Self-consciousness, which, as essential to all Experience, are not the result of any ; constituting in truth the Laws by which the possibility of our cognitive functions is determined. This process, by which we thus attain to a discrimi-

Par. XXI. Speculation, — as a means of Knowledge.

native knowledge of the *Necessary, Native,* and, as they are also called, the *Noetic, Pure, a priori,* or *Transcendental, Elements of Thought,* may be styled *Speculative Analysis, Analytic Speculation,* or *Speculation* simply, and is carefully to be distinguished from Induction, with which it is not unusually confounded.

Explication.

The empirical knowledge of which we have hitherto been speaking, does not, however varied and extensive it may be, suffice to satisfy the thinking mind as such; for our empirical knowledge itself points at certain higher cognitions from which it may obtain completion, and which are of a very different character from that by which the mere empirical cognitions themselves are distinguished. The cognitions are styled, among other names, by those of *noetic, pure,* or *rational,* and they are such as cannot, though manifested in experience, be derived from experience; for, as the conditions under which experience is possible, they must be viewed as necessary constituents of the nature of the thinking principle itself. Philosophers have indeed been found to deny the reality of such cognitions native to the mind; and to confine the whole sphere of human knowledge to the limits of experience. But in this case philosophers have overlooked the important circumstance, that the acts, that is, the apprehension and judgment, of experience, are themselves impossible, except under the supposition of certain potential cognitions previously existent in the thinking subject, and which become actual on occasion of an object being presented to the external or internal sense. As an example of a noetic cognition, the following propositions may suffice:— An object and all its attributes are convertible;—All that is has its sufficient cause. The principal distinctions of Empirical and Rational Knowledges, or rather Empirical and Noetic Cognitions, are the following:

<small>Principal distinctions of Empirical and Noetic Cognitions.</small> —1°, Empirical Cognitions originate exclusively in experience, whereas Noetic Cognitions are virtually at least before or above all experience,—all experience being only possible through them. 2°, Empirical cognitions come piecemeal and successively into existence, and may again gradually fade and disappear; whereas noetic cognitions, like Pallas, armed and immortal from the head of Jupiter, spring at once into existence, complete and indestructible. 3°, Empirical cognitions find only an application to these objects from which they were originally abstracted, and, according as things obtain a different form, they also may become differently fashioned; noetic cognitions, on the contrary, bear the character impressed on them of necessity, universality, sameness. Whether a cognition be empirical or noetic, can only be determined by considering whether it can or cannot be presented in a sensible perception;—whether it do or do not stand forward clear, distinct, and indestructible, bearing the stamp of necessity and absolute universality. The noetic cognitions can be detected only by a critical analysis of the mental phænomena proposed for the purpose of their discovery; and this analysis may, as I have said, be styled Speculation, for want of a more appropriate appellation.

LECTURE IX.—MODIFIED METHODOLOGY.

SECTION I.—OF THE ACQUISITION OF KNOWLEDGE.

III. COMMUNICATION OF KNOWLEDGE.—A. INSTRUC-
TION—ORAL AND WRITTEN.—B. CONFERENCE
—DIALOGUE AND DISPUTATION.

I NOW go on to the last Mean of Acquiring and Perfecting our knowledge ; and commence with the following paragraph :

¶ XXII. An important mean for the Acquisition and Perfecting of Knowledge is the Communication of Thought. Considered in general, the Communication of thought is either One-sided, or Mutual. The former is called *Instruction (institutio)*, the latter, *Conference (collocutio);* but these, though in theory distinct, are in practice easily combined. Instruction is again either *Oral* or *Written;* and Conference, as it is interlocutory and familiar, or controversial and solemn, may be divided into *Dialogue (colloquium, dialogus)*, and *Disputation (disputatio, concertatio).* The Communication of thought in all its forms is a means of intel-

Par. XXII. The Communication of Thought, — as a means of Acquiring and Perfecting Knowledge.

lectual improvement, not only to him who receives, but to him who bestows, information; in both relations, therefore, it ought to be considered, and not, as is usually done, in the former only.

Explication. In illustrating this paragraph, I shall commence with the last sentence, and, before treating in detail of Instruction and Conference, as means of extending the limits of our knowledge by new acquisitions derived from the communication of others, I shall endeavour to show, that the Communication of Thought is itself an important mean towards the perfecting of knowledge in the mind of the communicator himself. In this view, the communication of knowledge is like the attribute of mercy, twice blessed,—" blessed to him that gives and to him that takes;" in teaching others we in fact teach ourselves.

The Communication of Thought an Important mean towards the perfecting of Knowledge in the mind of the communicator.

This view of the reflex effect of the communication of thought on the mind, whether under the form of Instruction or of Conference, is one of high importance, but it is one which has, in modern times, unfortunately been almost wholly overlooked. To illustrate it in all its bearings would require a volume; at present I can only contribute a few hints towards its exposition.

Man is, by an original tendency of his nature, determined to communicate to others what occupies his thoughts, and by this communication he obtains a clearer understanding of the subject of his cogitations than he could otherwise have compassed. This fact did not escape the acuteness of Plato. In the *Protagoras*,—

Man naturally determined to communication.

This fact noticed by Plato.

10

"It has been well," says Plato (and he has had sundry passages to the point),—"It has been well, I think, observed by Homer—

'Through mutual intercourse and mutual aid,
Great deeds are done and great discoveries made;
The wise new wisdom on the wise bestow,
Whilst the lone thinker's thoughts come slight and slow.'

For in company we, all of us, are more alert, in deed and word and thought. *And if a man excogitate aught by himself, forthwith he goes about to find some one to whom he may reveal it, and from whom he may obtain encouragement, aye and until his discovery be completed.*" The same doctrine is maintained by Aristotle, and illustrated by the same quotation; (to which, indeed, is to be referred the adage,—"*Unus homo, nullus homo.*")—" We rejoice," says Themistius, " in hunting truth in company, as in hunting game." Lucilius,—"*Scire est nescire, nisi id me scire alius scierit;*" paraphrased in the compacter, though far inferior, verse of Persius,—"*Scire tuum nihil est, nisi te scire hoc sciat alter.*" Cicero's Cato testifies to the same truth :— "*Non facile est invenire, qui quod sciat ipse, non tradat alteri.*" And Seneca :— " *Sic cum hac exceptione detur sapientia, ut illam inclusam teneam nec enunciem, rejiciam. Nullius boni, sine socio, jucunda possessio est.*"

"*Condita tabescit, vulgata scientia crescit.*"
" *In hoc gaudeo aliquid discere, ut doceam: nec me ulla res delectabit, licet eximia sit et salutaris, quam mihi uni, sciturus sim.*" "*Ita non solum ad discendum propensi sumus, verum etiam ad docendum.*"

The modes in which the Communication of thought is conducive to the perfecting of thought itself, are two; for the mind may be determined to more exalted energy by the sympathy of society, and by the stimulus of opposition; or it may be necessitated to more distinct, accurate, and orderly thinking, as this is the condition of distinct, accurate, and orderly communication. Of these the former requires the presence of others during the act of thought, and is, therefore, only manifested in oral instruction or in conference: whereas the latter is operative both in our oral and in our written communications. Of these in their order.

Modes in which Communication is conducive to the Perfecting of Thought are two.

In the first place, then, the influence of man on man in reciprocally determining a higher energy of the faculties, is a phænomenon sufficiently manifest. By nature a social being, man has powers which are relative to, and, consequently, find their development in, the company of his fellows; and this is more particularly shown in the energies of the cognitive faculties. "As iron sharpeneth iron," says Solomon, "so a man sharpeneth the understanding of his friend." This, as I have said, is effected both by fellow-feeling and by opposition. We see the effects of fellow-feeling in the necessity of an audience to call forth the exertions of the orator. Eloquence requires numbers; and oratory has only flourished where the condition of large audiences has been supplied. But opposition is perhaps still more powerful than mere sympathy in calling out the resources of the intellect.

1. By reciprocally determining a higher energy of the faculties.
(a) Through sympathy.
(b) Through Opposition.

In the mental as well as in the material world, action and reäction are ever equal ; and Plutarch well observes, that as motion would cease were contention to be taken out of the physical universe, so progress in improvement would cease were contention taken out of the moral ; πόλεμος ἁπάντων πατήρ.

Plutarch.

"It is maintained," says the subtle Scaliger, "by Vives, that we profit more by silent meditation than by dispute. This is not true. For as fire is elicited by the collision of stones, so truth is elicited by the collision of minds. I myself (he adds) frequently meditate by myself long and intently ; but in vain ; unless I find an antagonist, there is no hope of a successful issue. By a master we are more excited than by a book ; but an antagonist, whether by his pertinacity or his wisdom, is to me a double master."

Scaliger, J. C.

But, in the second place, the necessity of communicating a piece of knowledge to others, imposes upon us the necessity of obtaining a fuller consciousness of that knowledge for ourselves. This result is to a certain extent secured by the very process of clothing our cogitations in words. For speech is an analytic process ; and to express our thoughts in language, it is requisite to evolve them from the implicit into the explicit, from the confused into the distinct, in order to bestow on each part of the organic totality of a thought its precise and appropriate symbol. But to do this is in fact only to accomplish the first step towards the perfecting of our cognitions or thoughts.

2. By imposing the necessity of obtaining a fuller consciousness of knowledge for ourselves.

But the communication of thought, in its higher applica-.

tions, imposes on us far more than this; and in so doing it reäcts with a still more beneficial influence on our habits of thinking. Suppose that we are not merely to express our thoughts as they spontaneously arise; suppose that we are not merely extemporaneously to speak, but deliberately to write, and that what we are to communicate is not a simple and easy, but a complex and difficult, matter. In this case, no man will ever fully understand his sub-

Influence of Composition and Instruction in perfecting our Knowledge.

ject who has not studied it with the view of communication, while the power of communicating a subject is the only competent criterion of his fully understanding

Godwin quoted.

it. " When a man," says Godwin, " writes a book of methodical investigation, he does not write because he understands the subject, but he understands the subject because he has written. He was an uninstructed tyro, exposed to a thousand foolish and miserable mistakes, when he began his work, compared with the degree of proficiency to which he has attained when he has finished it. He who is now an eminent philosopher, or a sublime poet, was formerly neither the one nor the other. Many a man has been overtaken by a premature death, and left nothing behind him but compositions worthy of ridicule and contempt, who, if he had lived, would perhaps have risen to the highest literary eminence. If we could examine the school exercises of men who have afterwards done honour to mankind, we should often find them inferior to those of their ordinary competitors. If we could dive into the portfolios of their early youth, we should meet with abundant matter for laughter at their senseless incongruities, and for contemptuous astonishment.

"The one exclusive sign," says Aristotle, "that a man is thoroughly cognizant of anything, is that he is able to teach it;" and Ovid,—

Aristotle.

"*Quodque parum novit nemo docere potest.*"

In this reäctive effect of the communication of knowledge in determining the perfection of the knowledge communicated, originated the scholastic maxim *Doce ut discas*,—a maxim which has unfortunately been too much overlooked in the schemes of modern education. In former ages, *teach that you may learn* always constituted one at least of the great means of intellectual cultivation. "To teach," says Plato, "is the way for a man to learn most and best." "*Homines dum docent discunt*," says Seneca. "In teaching," says Clement of Alexandria, "the instructor often learns more than his pupils." "*Disce sed a doctis; indoctos ipse doceto*," is the precept of Dionysius Cato; and the two following were maxims of authority in the discipline of the middle ages. The first—

Plato.
Seneca.

Clement of Alexandria.
Dionysius Cato.

"*Multa rogare, rogata tenere, retenta docere,*
Haec tria, discipulum faciunt superare magistrum."

The second—

"*Discere si quaeris doceas; sic ipse doceris;*
Nam studio tali tibi proficis atque sodali."

This truth is also well enforced by the great Vives. "*Doctrina est traditio eorum quae quis novit ei qui non novit. Disciplina est illius traditionis acceptio; nisi quod mens accipientis impletur, dantis vero non exhauritur,—imo communicatione augetur eruditio,*

Vives.

sicut ignis, motu atque agitatione. Excitatur enim ingenium, et discurrit per ea quae ad præsens negotium pertinent: ita invenit atque excudit multa, et quae in mentem non veniebant cessanti, docenti, aut disserenti occurunt, calore acuente vigorem ingenii. Idcirco, nihil est ad magnam eruditionem perinde conducens, ut docere." The celebrated logician,

<small>Sanderson.</small>

Dr. Robert Sanderson, used to say: "I learn much from my master, more from my equals, and most of all from my disciples."

But I have occupied perhaps too much time on the influence of the communication of know-

<small>Influence of the communication of Knowledge on those to whom it is addressed.</small>

ledge on those by whom it is made; and shall now pass on to the consideration of its influence on those to whom it is addressed. And in treating of communication in this respect, I shall, in the first place, consider it as One-sided, and, in the second, as Reciprocal or Bilateral.

The Unilateral Communication of knowledge, or Instruction, is of two kinds, for it is either Oral or Written; but as both these species of instruction propose the same end, they are both, to a certain extent, subject to

<small>1. Instruction,— Oral and Written.</small>

the same laws.

Oral and Written Instruction have each their peculiar advantages.

In the first place, instruction by the living voice has this advantage over that of books, that, as more

<small>Oral instruction,— its advantages.
(a) More natural, therefore more impressive.
Theophrastus.</small>

natural, it is more impressive. Hearing rouses the attention and keeps it alive far more effectually than reading. To this we have the testimony of the most competent observers. "Hearing," says Theophrastus, " is of all the senses the most pathetic," that is, it is the sense most intimately associated with sentiment and passion.

Younger Pliny. "*Multo magis,*" says the Younger Pliny, "*multo magis* viva vox *afficit. Nam, licet acriora sunt quæ legas, altius tamen in animo sedent quæ pronuntiatio, vultus, habitus, gestus etiam dicentis adfigit.*"

"*Plus prodest,*" says Valerius Maximus, "docentem *Valerius Maximus.* audiere, *quam in libris studere; quia vehementior fit impressio in mentibus audientium, ex visu doctoris et auditu, quam ex studio et libro.*"

And St. Jerome—"*Habet nescio quid latentis energiæ* viva vox; *et in aures discipuli de doctoris St. Jerome. ore transfusa, fortius sonat.*"

A second reason why our Attention (and Memory is always in the ratio of Attention) to things (b) Less permanent spoken is greater than to things read, is therefore more attended to. that what is written we regard as a permanent possession to which we can always recur at pleasure; whereas we are conscious that the "winged words" are lost to us forever, if we do not catch them as they fly. As Pliny hath it: "*Legendi semper est occasio; audiendi non semper.*"

A third cause of the superior efficacy of oral instruction is that man is a social animal. He is thus naturally disposed to find pleasure in society, and in the performance of the actions performed by those with whom he consorts. But reading is a solitary, hearing is a social act. In reading, we are not determined to attend by any fellow-feeling with others attending; whereas in hearing, our (c) Hearing a social act. attention is not only engaged by our sympathy with the speaker, but by our sympathy with the other attentive auditors around us.

Such are the causes which concur in rendering Oral

Instruction more effectual than Written. "M. Varillas,"
says Menage (and Varillas was one of the most learned of modern historians,- and Menage one of the most learned of modern scholars), "M. Varillas himself told me one day, that of every ten things he knew, he had learned nine of them in conversation. I myself might say nearly the same thing."

Menage quoted.

On the other hand, Reading, though only a substitute for Oral Instruction, has likewise advantages peculiar to itself. In the first place, it is more easily accessible. In the second, it is more comprehensive in its sphere of operation. In the third, it is not transitory with the voice, but may again and again be taken up and considered, so that the object of the instruction may thus more fully be examined and brought to proof. It is thus manifest, that oral and written instruction severally supply and severally support each other; and that, where this is competent, they ought always to be employed in conjunction. Oral instruction is, however, in the earlier stages of education, of principal importance; and written ought, therefore, at first only to be brought in as a subsidiary. A neglect of the oral instruction, and an exclusive employment of the written,—the way in which those who are self-taught (the autodidacti) obtain their education,—for the most part betrays its one-sided influence by a contracted cultivation of the intellect, with a deficiency in the power of communicating knowledge to others.

Reading,—its advantages.
(a) More easily accessible.
(b) More comprehensive.
(c) More permanent.

Oral instruction necessarily supposes a speaker and a hearer; and written instruction a writer and a reader. In these, the capacity of the speaker and of the writer must equally fulfil certain common requisites. In the first place, they should be fully masters of the subject with which their instruction is conversant; and in the second, they should be able and willing to communicate to others the knowledge which they themselves possess. But in reference to these several species of instruction, there are various special rules that ought to be attended to by those who would reap the advantages they severally afford. I shall commence with Written Instruction, and comprise the rules by which it ought to be regulated, in the following paragraph.

¶ XXIII. In regard to Written Instruction, and its profitable employment as a means of intellectual improvement, there are certain rules which ought to be observed, and which together constitute the Proper Method of Reading.

Par. XXIII. Written Instruction, and its employment as a means of intellectual improvement.

These may be reduced to three classes, as they regard, 1°, The Quantity, 2°, The Quality, of what is to be read, or, 3°, The Mode of Reading what is to be read.

I. As concerns the Quantity of what is to be read, there is a single rule,—read much, but not many works *(multum non multa)*.

II. As concerns the Quality of what is to be read,— there may be given five rules, 1°, Select the works of principal importance, estimated by relation to the several sciences themselves, or to your particular aim in reading, or to your individual disposition and wants. 2°, Read not the more detailed works upon a science, until you have obtained a rudimentary knowledge of it in general. 3°, Make yourselves familiar with a science in its actual or present state, before you proceed to study it in its chronological development. 4°, To avoid erroneous and exclusive views, read and compare together the more important works of every sect and party. 5°, To avoid a one-sided development of mind, combine with the study of works which cultivate the Understanding, the study of works which cultivate the Taste.

III. As concerns the Mode or Manner of reading itself, there are four principal rules. 1°, Read that you may accurately remember, but still more, that you may fully understand. 2°, Strive to compass the general tenor of a work, before you attempt to judge of it in detail. 3°, Accommodate the intensity of the reading to the importance of the work. Some books are, therefore, to be only dipped into; others are to be run over rapidly; and others to be studied long and sedulously. 4°, Regulate on the same principle the extracts which you make from the works you read.

I. In reference to the head of Quantity, the single rule is—Read much, but not many works. Though this golden rule has risen in importance, since the world, by the art of printing, has been overwhelmed by the multitude of books, it was still fully recognized by the great thinkers of antiquity. It is even hinted by Solomon, when he complains that "of making many books there is no end." By Quintillian, by the younger Pliny, and by Seneca, the maxim, "*multum legendum esse, non multa,*" is laid down as the great rule of study. "All," says Luther in his Table Talk, "who would study with advantage in any art whatsoever, ought to betake

Explication.
I. Quantity to be read.
Rule.
Solomon.
Quintillian.
Younger Pliny.
Seneca.
Luther quoted.

themselves to the reading of some sure and certain books oftentimes over; for to read many books produceth confusion, rather than learning, like as those who dwell everywhere, are not anywhere at home." He alludes here to the saying of Seneca, "*Nusquam est qui ubique est.*" And like as in society, we use not daily the community of all our acquaintances, but of some few selected friends, even so likewise ought we to accustom ourselves to the best books, and to make the same familiar unto us, that is, to have them, as we used to say, at our finger ends. The great

Sanderson. logician, Bishop Sanderson, to whom I formerly referred, as his friend and biographer Isaac Walton informs us, said "that he declined reading many books; but what he did read were well chosen, and read so often that he became very familiar with them. They were principally three,—Aristotle's *Rhetoric*, Aquinas's *Secunda Secundæ*, and Cicero, particularly his

Lord Burleigh. *Offices*." The great Lord Burleigh, we are told by his biographer, carried Cicero *De Officiis*, with Aristotle's *Rhetoric*, always in his bosom; these being complete pieces, "that would make both a scholar and an honest man." "Our age,"

Herder. says Herder, "is the reading age;" and he adds, "it would have been better, in my opinion, for the world and for science, if, instead of the multitude of books which now overlay us, we possessed only a few works good and sterling, and which, as few, would, therefore, be more diligently and profoundly studied." I might quote to you many other testimonies to the same effect; but testimonies are useless in support of so manifest a truth.

For what purpose,—with what intent, do we read? We read not for the sake of reading, but we read to the end that we may think. Reading is valuable only as it may supply to us the materials which the mind itself elaborates. As it is not the largest quantity of any kind of food, taken into the stomach, that conduces to health, but such a quantity of such a kind as can be best digested; so it is not the greatest complement of any kind of information that improves the mind, but such a quantity of such a kind as determines the intellect to most vigorous energy. The only profitable reading is that in which we are compelled to think, and think intensely; whereas that reading which serves only to dissipate and divert our thought, is either positively hurtful, or useful only as an occasional relaxation from severe exertion. But the amount of vigorous thinking is usually in the inverse ratio of multifarious reading. Multifarious reading is agreeable; but, as a habit, it is, in its way, as destructive to the mental as dram-drinking is to the bodily health.

End of Reading.

II. In reference to the Quality of what is to be read, the First of the five rules is—" Select the works of principal importance, in accommodation either to the several sciences themselves, or to your particular aim in reading, or to your individual disposition and wants. This rule is too manifestly true to require any illustration of its truth. No one will deny that for the accomplishment of an end you ought to employ the means best calculated for its accomplishment. This is all that the rule inculcates. But while there is no difficulty about the expediency of obeying the rule, there is often considerable difficulty in obeying it. To know what books ought to be read in order to learn a science, is in fact frequently obtained after the science has been already learned. On this point no

II. Quality of what is to be read.
First Rule.

general advice can be given. We have, on all of the sciences, works which profess to supply the advice which the student here requires. But in general, I must say, they are of small assistance in pointing out what books we should select, however useful they may be in showing us what books exist upon a science. In this respect, the British student also labours under peculiar disadvantages. The libraries in this country are, one and all of them, wretchedly imperfect; and there are few departments of science in which they are not destitute even of the works of primary necessity,—works which, from their high price, but more frequently from the difficulty of procuring them, are beyond the reach of ordinary readers.

Under the head of Quality the Second Rule is—"Read not the more detailed works upon a science, until you have obtained a rudimentary knowledge of it in general." The expediency of this rule is sufficiently apparent. It is altogether impossible to read with advantage an extensive work on any branch of knowledge, if we are not previously aware of its general bearing, and of the relations in which its several parts stand to each other. In this case, the mind is overpowered and oppressed by the mass of details presented to it,—details, the significance and subordination of which it is as yet unable to recognize. A conspectus,—a survey of the science as a whole, ought, therefore, to precede the study of it in its parts; we should be aware of its distribution, before we attend to what is distributed,—we should possess the empty frame-work, before we collect the materials with which it is to be filled. Hence the utility of an encyclopædical knowledge of the sciences in general, preliminary to a study of the several sciences in particular; that is, a summary knowledge of their objects, their extent, their connection with each other. By this means the student is enabled to steer his way on the wide ocean of science. By this means he always knows whereabouts he is, and becomes aware of the point towards which his author is leading him.

In entering upon the study of such authors as Plato, Aristotle, Descartes, Spinoza, Leibnitz, Locke, Kant, etc., it is, therefore, proper that we first obtain a preparatory acquaintance with the scope, both of their philosophy in general, and of the particular work on which we are about to enter. In the case of writers of such ability this is not difficult to do, as there are abundance of subsidiary works, affording the preliminary knowledge of which we are in quest. But in the case of treatises where similar assistance is not at hand, we may often, in some degree, prepare ourselves for a regular perusal, by examining the table of contents, and taking a cursory inspection of its several departments. In this respect, and also in others, the following advice of

Gibbon quoted. Gibbon to young students is highly deserving of attention. " After a rapid glance (I translate from the original French)—after a rapid glance on the subject and distribution of a new book, I suspend the reading of it, which I only resume after having myself examined the subject in all its relations,—after having called up in my solitary walks all that I have read, thought, or learned in regard to the subject of the whole book, or of some chapter in particular. I thus place myself in a condition to estimate what the author may add to my general stock of knowledge ; and I am thus sometimes favorably disposed by the accordance, sometimes armed by the opposition,-of our views.

The third Rule under the head of Quality is—"Make yourselves familiar with a science in its present state, before you proceed to study it in its chronological development." The propriety of this procedure is likewise manifest. Unless we be acquainted with a science in its more advanced state, it is impossible to distinguish between what is more or less important, and, consequently, impossible to determine what is or is not worthy of attention in the doctrines of its earlier cultivators. We shall thus also be overwhelmed by the infinitude of details successively presented to us; all will be confusion and darkness where all ought to be order and light. It is thus improper to study philosophy historically, or in its past progress, before we have studied it statistically, or in its actual results.

<small>Third Rule.</small>

The Fourth Rule under the same head is—"To avoid erroneous and exclusive views, read and compare together the more important works of every party." In proportion as different opinions may be entertained in regard to the objects of a science, the more necessary is it that we should weigh with care and impartiality the reasons on which these different opinions rest. Such a science, in particular, is philosophy, and such sciences, in general, are those which proceed out of philosophy. In the philosophical sciences, we ought, therefore, to be especially on our guard against that partiality which considers only the arguments in favor of particular opinions. It is true that in the writings of one party we find adduced the reasons of the opposite party; but frequently so distorted, so mutilated, so enervated, that their refutation occasions little effort. We must, therefore, study the arguments on both sides, if we would avoid those one-sided and contracted

<small>Fourth Rule.</small>

views which are the result of party-spirit. The precept of the Apostle, "Test all things, hold fast by that which is good," is a precept which is applicable equally in philosophy as in theology, but a precept that has not been more frequently neglected in the one study than in the other.

The Fifth Rule under the head of Quality is—"To avoid a one-sided development of mind, combine with the study of works which cultivate the Understanding, the study of works which cultivate the Taste." The propriety of this rule requires no elucidation;

Fifth Rule.

I, therefore, pass on to the third head— viz., the manner of reading itself; under which the First Rule is—"Read that you may accurately remember, but still more that you may fully understand."

III. Manner of Reading.
First Rule.

This also requires no comment. Reading should not be a learning by rote, but an act of reflective thinking. Memory is only a subsidiary faculty,—is valuable merely as supplying the materials on which the understanding is to operate. We read, therefore, principally, not to remember facts, but to understand relations. To commit, therefore, to memory what we read, before we elaborate it into an intellectual possession, is not only useless but detrimental; for the habit of laying up in memory what has not been digested by the understanding, is at once the cause and the effect of mental weakness.

The Second Rule under this head is—"Strive to compass the general tenor of a work, before you attempt to judge of it in detail." Nothing can be more absurd than the attempt to judge a part before comprehending the whole; but unfortunately nothing is

Second Rule.

more common, especially among professional critics,—reviewers. This proceeding is, however, as frequently the effect of wilful misrepresentation, as of unintentional error.

<small>Third Rule.</small> The Third Rule under this head is—"Accommodate the intensity of the reading to the importance of the work. Some books are, therefore, to be only dipped into; others are to be run over rapidly; and others to be studied long and sedulously." All books are not to be read with the same attention; and, accordingly, an ancient distinction was taken of reading into *lectio cursoria* and *lectio stataria*. The former of these we have adopted into English, cursorary reading being a familiar and correct translation of *lectio cursoria*. But *lectio stataria* cannot be so well rendered by the expression of *stationary reading*.

<small>Lectio cursoria. Lectio stataria.</small>

<small>Bacon quoted.</small> "Read not," says Bacon, in his Fiftieth Essay—"read not to contradict and confute, nor to believe and take for granted, nor to find talk and discourse, but to weigh and consider. Some books are to be tasted, others are to be swallowed, and some few to be chewed and digested; that is, some books are to be read only in parts; others to be read, but not curiously; and some few to be read wholly and with diligence and attention. Some books also may be read by deputy, and extracts made of them by others; but that would be only in the less important arguments, and the meaner sort of books; else distilled books are, like common distilled waters, fleshy things." "One kind of book," says the great historian, Johann von Müller, " I read with great rapidity, for in these there is much dross

<small>Johann von Müller.</small>

COMMUNICATION OF KNOWLEDGE. 211

to throw aside, and little gold to be found ; some, however, there are all gold and diamonds, and he who, for example, in Tacitus can read more than twenty pages in four hours, certainly does not understand him."

Rapidity in reading depends, however, greatly on our acquaintance with the subject of discussion. At first, upon a science we can only read with profit few books, and laboriously. By degrees, however, our knowledge of the matters treated expands, the reasonings appear more manifest, —we advance more easily, until at length we are able, without overlooking anything of importance, to read with a velocity which appears almost incredible for those who are only commencing the study.

The Fourth Rule under this head is—" Regulate on the same principle the extracts which you make from the works you read.

Fourth Rule.

So much for the Unilateral Communication of thought, as a mean of knowledge. We now proceed to the Mutual Communication of thought,—Conference.

This is either mere Conversation,—mere Dialogue, or Formal Dispute, and at present we consider both of these exclusively only as a means of knowledge,—only as a means for the communication of truth.

Conference,—of two kinds.

The employment of Dialogue as such a mean, requires great skill and dexterity ; for presence of mind, confidence, tact, and pliability are necessary for this, and these are only obtained by exercise, independently of natural talent. This was the method which Socrates almost exclusively employed in the communication of knowledge ; and he called it his *art of intellectual midwifery,*

1. Dialogue.

because in its application truth is not given over by the master to the disciple, but the master, by skilful questioning, only helps the disciple to deliver himself of the truth explicity, which his mind had before held implicitly. This method is not, however, applicable to all kinds of knowledge, but only to those which the human intellect is able to evolve out of itself, that is, only to the cognitions of Pure Reason. Disputation is of two principal kinds, inasmuch as it is oral or written ; and in both cases, the controversy may be conducted either by the rules of strict logical disputation, or left to the freedom of debate. Without entering on details, it may be sufficient to state, in regard to

<small>2. Disputation,— Oral and Written. Academical disputation.</small>

Logical disputation, that it is here essential that the point in question,—the *status controversiæ*,—the thesis, should, in the first place, be accurately determined, in order to prevent all logomachy, or mere verbal wrangling. This being done, that disputant who denies the thesis, and who is called the *opponent*, may either call upon the disputant who affirms the thesis, and who is called the *defendant*, to allege an argument in its support, or he may at once himself produce his counter-argument. To avoid, however, all misunderstanding, the opponent should also advance an antithesis, that is, a proposition conflictive with the thesis, and when this has been denied by the defendant the process of argumentation commences. This proceeds in regular syllogisms, and is governed by definite rules, which are all so calculated that the discussion is not allowed to wander from the point at issue, and each disputant is compelled, in reference to every syllogism of his adversary, either to admit, or to deny, or to distinguish. These rules you will find in most of the older systems of Logic; in particular I may refer you to them as detailed in Heerebord's *Praxis Logica*, to be found at the end of his edition of the *Synopsis* of Burgersdicius. The practice of disputation was long and justly regarded as the most important of academical exercises; though liable to abuse, the good which it certainly ensures greatly surpasses the evil which it may accidentally occasion.

THE END.

www.ingramcontent.com/pod-product-compliance
Lightning Source LLC
Chambersburg PA
CBHW031828230426
43669CB00009B/1263